GETTING THE MONEY

GETTING THE MONEY

How to Succeed in Fundraising for Public and Nonprofit Libraries

Ken Dowlin

LIBRARIES UNLIMITED
A Member of the Greenwood Publishing Group
Westport, Connecticut • London

Library of Congress Cataloging-in-Publication Data

Dowlin, Kenneth E.
  Getting the money : how to succeed in fundraising for public and nonprofit libraries / Ken Dowlin.
      p.   cm.
  Includes bibliographical references and index.
  ISBN 978–1–59158–597–8 (alk. paper)
  1. Library fund raising—United States.   2. Library fund raising.   3. Public libraries—United States—Finance.   4. Public libraries—Finance.   5. Libraries and community.   I. Title.
  Z683.2.U6D69   2009
  025.1′1—dc22   2008022887

British Library Cataloguing in Publication Data is available.

Copyright © 2009 by Ken Dowlin

All rights reserved. No portion of this book may be reproduced, by any process or technique, without the express written consent of the publisher.

Library of Congress Catalog Card Number: 2008022887
ISBN: 978–1–59158–597–8

First published in 2009

Libraries Unlimited, 88 Post Road West, Westport, CT 06881
A Member of the Greenwood Publishing Group, Inc.
www.lu.com

Printed in the United States of America

The paper used in this book complies with the
Permanent Paper Standard issued by the National
Information Standards Organization (Z39.48–1984).

10 9 8 7 6 5 4 3 2 1

Contents

Preface		xi
Acknowledgments		xiii
	Introduction	1
1.	**Getting Them Hungry (Putting Out the Bait)**	5
	Need for Change	5
	Communicating with Stakeholders	6
	Raising Expectations	6
	Surveying Your Community	8
	Identifying Stakeholders and Linking Communications	10
2.	**Cleaning Out the Kitchen**	11
	Minimizing Dysfunctional Myths	11
	Assessing Effectiveness and Efficiency	15
	Getting Rid of the Baggage	17
	Minimizing the Negative Rumor Mill	17
	Clarify and Codify Policies, Procedures, Feedback, and Control System	18
	Educate and Inform the Staff	18
3.	**Organizing the Kitchen (Strategic Thinking)**	21
	Personal Knowledge and Skills Development	21
	Develop Your Own Vision, Values, Mission, and Even Dreams for the Library	22
	Do Your Homework	22
	Build Your Case Statement	22
	Learn to Observe and Chart Group Dynamics in Meetings	23
	Learn to Learn	24

Learn to Educate Others	24
Learn to Present	25
Stories about Yourself, Your Organization, and Your Goals	27
Understanding Financial Management Realities	27
Determine Your Authority	28
Analyzing Your Community	28
Elected Officials	28
Users	29
Community Organizations	29
Making Cities Stronger	30
Natural Stakeholders	31
Organizations That Want to Ride Your Publicity Coat Tails	31
Donors	32
Identify the Barriers	32
Financial Limitations	32
Knowing Who to Talk to When	34
Understand the Impact of Change	34
Graphic to Neographic Content	34
Singular Processes to Mass Processes	35
Mono Access to Multidimensional Access Points	35
Single to Many Simultaneous Users	35
Singular to Collaborative Organizations	36
Ownership Orientation to Access Orientation	36
Rights of Ownership to Licensing and Stricter Copyright	36
Government Mandates	36
Self-Service	37
Experiential Library	37
Gatekeeper to Facilitator	38
Fortress to Pipeline	38
Frey's Thesis	38
The Internet World	39
Get Your Vision Out to the Public	39
Team Building	39
Creating the Learning Organization	40
Personnel Management	41
Change Management	41
Strategic Planning	42
Build a "Go-to-Team"	43
Media Relations	44
Understanding and Cultivating Relationships	45
Differences in Groups or Organizations	45
Development Departments of Parent Organization	46
Museums	46
Library Schools or Other Schools with Student Resources	46
Corporate Leaders and Influential Citizens	46
Local Foundations	47
Angels	47
Muscle People	47

	Devils	47
	Leadership and Support for Formal Support Groups	48
	External Organization Development	48
	Create New Stakeholders	49
	Build Alliances with Stakeholders	49
	Build Alliances with Neighborhood Organizations	50
	Final Kitchen Cleaning	50
4.	**Getting Good Equipment: Skillets, Pots and Pans, Knives, and Cookbooks**	51
	Community Relations Office (CRO)	52
	Formal Support Groups	53
	Friends of the Library	53
	Library Foundation	54
	Junior Friends	55
	Staff Associations	55
	Volunteers	55
	Staff	56
	Communication Tools and Techniques	56
	Branding	58
	Advocacy	59
	Media Storm Firefighting	61
	Testimonials	62
	Anecdotes	63
	Rethinking Your Look	63
	Dealing with the News Media	64
	Toolkit with the News Media	66
	Finding Cookbooks	68
	Fundraising and Development	68
	Happy Cooking	69
5.	**Nibbles and Starter Recipes**	71
	Community Organization Presentations	72
	Book Sales	73
	Sponsored Book Fairs	74
	Cookbooks	74
	Naming Opportunities	74
	Bookplates	75
	Donated Subscriptions	75
	Service or Product Donations	76
	Public Programming	76
	Golf Tournament and Baseball Games	77
	Fees for Services	77
	Small Community Foundation Grants	78
	Partnerships with Other Cultural Institutions	78
	Partnerships with Fellow Government Agencies	79
	Charitable Planned Giving	79
	Remainder Trusts	79

Wills and Bequests	79
Direct Mail Campaigns	80
Endowments	80
State Funding	80
Federal Funding	82
Innovative Commercial Approaches	82
Credit Card Programs	82
Transit Companies	82
Stay in the Library Forever	83
Creative Projects with Dedicated Supporters	83
Raising Money Online	84

6. Holiday Menus (Strategies to Get Major Funds) — 87

Marketing Campaign Themes	88
Collection Excellence	89
Channels beyond the Print Collection	89
Funding New Technology	89
Public Programming	90
Building Campaigns	90
Diversity	92
Community Building	92
Go for Excellence	93
Private Funding Campaigns	93
Corporate or Business Approaches	94
Major Capital Campaigns	94
Family Foundations	95
Library Foundations	95
Community Foundations	95
Affinity Groups	96
Government Sources	96
Online Funding	96
Local Referendums	97
Tax Limitation Overrides	98
Increasing Statutory Limitations	98
Bond Issues	99
Revenue Entitlements	100
Running Campaigns for Referendums	101
Getting Started	101
Researching and Obtaining Legal Support and Authority	102
Creating the Case Statement	103
Expanding the Go-to-Team	104
Creating a Separate Campaign Committee	105
Polls	105
Consultants	106
Endorsements	106
Gaining Momentum	107
Getting the Money for the Campaign	107
Speakers' Bureau	108

	Door-to-Door Campaigning	108
	Telephone Banks	109
	Opposition	109
	In the Home Stretch	110
	Down to the Wire	110
	Closing Out	110
7.	**The Keys to the Financial Castle Kitchen**	**111**
	Strategic Thinking and Focus	111
	Always Selling Yourself and the Library	114
	Use Creative Ways to Get Publicity	114
	KISS	114
	Create a Must-Visit List	115
	Selling with Sizzle	115
	Star Power	115
	Leveraging Funding	115
	Building Relationships	116
	Community Connectedness	116
	Bring in Outside Talent to the Project	117
	People with Clout	117
	People Who Care	118
	Scout for Talent Outside Your Community	118
	Political Savvy	118
	Nurturing Political Leaders	119
	Build a Constituency	120
	Build on Success	120
	Family Celebrations	120
	Building a Reputation for Success	121
	Leveraging Assets	121
	The Mixed Revenues Approach	121
	Producing Proposals for Starter Funding	121
	Find the Talent	121
	Conceptual Visioning	122
	Create a Buzz	122
	Managing the Process	123
	Communications Program	123
	Donor Management Program	124
	Decision Support Program	125
	MyLibrary	125
	OurLibrary	126
	Just Do It	128
Appendix		**129**
Bibliography		**139**
Index		**143**

Preface

Although I was a dreamer as a youngster it never occurred to me that I would go so far from the world of the small town where I grew up in Colorado and I end up living in two of the largest metropolitan regions in the country (San Francisco and Los Angeles). That small town only had 250 inhabitants (I am still convinced that they counted the dogs to get that number for the highway sign). On days that I was driving a tractor in the hay fields my mind would wander building wonderful futures for myself. Occasionally an airplane would fly over and I would try to imagine who was on that plane, where were they from, and where are they going. I would dream that I was on that plane going off to a wonderful future. It seemed like joining the Marine Corp was the ticket to see the world at that time; but I diverted from that goal after taking a job on a bookmobile to pay my way through college. At that time I did not know that I would travel the world on behalf of libraries and people's access to information. I did realize early about the magic of libraries to not only entertain and educate, but to change people, their communities, and perhaps the world.

I was able to increase library services for millions of people. I am very proud of my opportunities and abilities. I am now convinced that my quest was, and still is, the eradication of ignorance. Most all ills in our societies and civilizations come from ignorance. I have not achieved my quest yet, and probably never will, but I do feel confident that a dent was made. On the personal level, I was able to finish three college degrees and participate in numerous learning opportunities throughout my career. Learning is a way of life for me and my family.

My epiphany that led to perhaps my greatest discovery did not come until late in my career. While designing the new main library at San Francisco Public Library (SFPL) the design team including me spent ten days in Europe learning from visits to major libraries and presentations by library colleagues. On the return home the two main architects, Kathy Simon and James Ingo Freed, and I were energized about the project. Ingo started drawing out the design concepts for the building on an airline napkin and we worked at verbalizing our goal. We knew we wanted a great library building that could become a great public building as well as the heart of a great library but we wanted more. I remembered that there was a book titled *The Soul of a New Machine* about the team that build one of the first mini computers (Kidder, 2000). I proposed that we should build a library with a soul and they all agreed that would be our ultimate goal. But, as I talked to people about that vision I started to wonder about what that phrase really meant. What is the soul of a library?

It didn't come to me until we had the party commemorating the closing of the old library. As I looked out at the hundreds and hundreds of people who were with us to celebrate, I tried to come up with a phrase about the library with a soul. Just before my time to thank them for all of their work, it hit me. *The soul of the library comes from the people who use it, support it, and love it.* Martin Paley, the executive director of the SFPL Foundation, validated that it was the affinity groups that was the capstone to the effort to involve stakeholders in the future of the library. The involvement of thousands of people brought the soul to the library (Bailey, 1994).

Acknowledgments

This book is dedicated to the many champions with whom I have had the privilege and joy of working with in my career. They are unselfish in their time, money, and support for a shared vision of what libraries can be. The list of champions could go on and on but here are some who really made a difference.

First, my wife who should have an honorary degree in library science needs recognition for her constant support in my many activities. She has been supportive for over forty-six years and we plan to keep going a long time. She not only supported me in my jobs—she had her own career in the medical field—but encouraged me to continue my education, and was the point person in raising two sons of whom we couldn't be more proud.

Nadine Moderhak and Jeanne Coffey at the Adams County Public Library helped convince me that libraries and librarianship were the career of choice. John Eastlick and Henry Shearouse at the Denver Public Library provided role models as library leaders. At the Arvada Public Library, Elizabeth Schroeder was a true champion. Within five years the library's budget was doubled, a new library was built, and library usage increased dramatically. It was a good setting for learning about the broader aspects of librarianship such as politics, the community connection, and getting money.

The Natrona County Public Library (NCPL) had a host of champions including Jim Crawford, Frank Bowron, John Albanese, Lois Schickich, and others. At the Pikes Peak Regional Library District (PPLD) Forest Bohart and his son Mike were tireless in their contribution to the library. Many members of the Friends of the Library (FOL) were also energetic and supportive. Bob and Dee Berry were outstanding examples of people supporting the cause at PPLD but there were many others who contributed.

In San Francisco the library had three angels who worked tirelessly for over forty years to make the library better. Marjorie Stern showed the most passion about the cause. It was her determination that led me to take the job as City Librarian for San Francisco in the first place. Mary Louise Stong was steadfast in her effort. Mig Meyer as Executive Director of the San Francisco Public Library (SFPL) Friends of the Library (FOL) was just as tireless. Mig was an excellent arranger and managed the Friends activities very well. Marjorie was constantly introducing me to people and groups that she felt I should know and who should know me. The first months on the job were an endless circle of meeting people. Fortunately, as it worked out she had many friends in high places and wasn't above nagging them when she felt it was needed. She was passionate about what she did and one of her pieces of advice was to never trust anyone who wasn't passionate about their cause.

The three of them were constant in their belief in the value of a great public library in their city and beyond. They convinced many people that the vision for the library should be high and they energized many people. Marjorie's vision was no small dream. She loved the New York Public Library (NYPL) and wanted SFPL to get to that level. She even convinced the dramatic leader of the renaissance of the NYPL, Vartan Gregorian, who is now president of the Carnegie Corporation of New York, to come to SFPL and help get the important people excited. Another angel who might not realize it was Robert Fisher of the San Francisco Foundation who was a critical financial catalyst for the new main library (NML) project. In San Francisco the list of leaders and supporters is huge.

The staff members who managed the public relations programs for these libraries were major contributors to the success of the libraries. In Arvada the wife of a newspaper sports reporter who was hired to write and place stories about the library demonstrated the value of good PR expertise to the librarians in the area. At NCPL Mary Hales brought experience in PR on the staff. Susan Watkins at PPLD got the program going there and Nancy Milvid was outstanding during the innovative years of the 1980s. At SFPL Marcia Schneider was working as a librarian when she volunteered to head the Community Relations Office (CRO). Marcia did an outstanding job during the 1990s and is still very effective for the library.

This book is also dedicated to those who will be the library leaders in the future. Many of the students at the San Jose State University (SJSU) School of Library and Information Science (SLIS) will be among them.

Introduction

This book is about fundraising. While it sounds like it would be a pretty easy topic to cover, a quick Google search on library fundraising brings up 7,550,000 hits. If the search is expanded to library development or similar terms the number of hits will be even more staggering. You certainly can't cover all of these in a lifetime, let alone a book. They run the gamut from online journal articles, proceedings from conferences, workshops, Web-based sites, to books. The content ranges from tips for community programs to attract new users, to strategies for increasing usage by current users, and to enlisting stakeholders in the effort to increase funding and other resources. This book focuses on weaving all of these activities together in a strategic funding program to grow the library's resources and services.

It is a systemic approach rather than a detailed one. There are natural activities such as story hours and book sales (a socially acceptable way to clean house of outdated, little used, or those orphan books that people leave on your doorstep while making a little money as well), and big-time bond or referendum issues for increased or dedicated funding. The top of the scale is a voter mandate to get long-term entitlement funding. While entitlement funding is rare, it does happen. There are insights from a variety of sources and a great deal of knowledge gained from personal experience brought together to provide a comprehensive picture rather than a detailed one.

This experience includes positions as director of libraries that are entities of a city, a county, a regional library district, and a city/county. The funding mechanisms and opportunities in each of these types of libraries are different due to different funding statutes or regulations. This experience provided unique knowledge about politics, the use of information technology for development purposes, and fundraising. There are also significant differences in development for small libraries and large ones.

A person will find that they will be more immersed in one of the three areas (politics, technology, and fundraising) than the others and they need to develop a sense of priority, which is also cognizant of their symbiotic relationship. This knowledge can prove to be the key to extending and enhancing library services to communities.

The focus is on a strategic fund development program, not just activities. The ability to raise funds from private sources, grants from other governmental entities, and activities of subsidiary groups is important in order to create a diversified funding stream. Many people understand this need, but few seem to understand that leveraging the small and flexible funding can lead to the big payoff. The big payoff comes through bond issues or funding increases through the political process for publicly funded libraries. Each activity needs to be considered for its ability to support the mission and vision of the organization through leverage funding and stakeholder development.

In organizational planning it is easy to create laundry lists of activities that we must do, need to do, or want to do. The crunch time comes when it is necessary to aggregate the activities into goals and strategies, to evaluate the success or failure of each type of activity, assign priorities, and to keep moving the program toward the end goal.

A successful public library leader knows their community's needs and dreams, creates a shared vision, and makes all people in the community see themselves as stakeholders in the success of the library. This leader is also a manager who creates a plan for the path forward, develops the implementation plan to get it all going, brings in the necessary talent and funding, and keeps the program on course.

While many librarians understand that going to the voters or elected officials is a political process, they don't realize the importance for the library to be active at politics and that librarians have a personal and professional responsibility to ensure that the library will be successful in politics. Some librarians think that they shouldn't have anything to do with politics. There seems to be an assumption that what we do is virtuous and we shouldn't have to sell our library or ourselves.

Skills in politics are very important to the librarians on more than one front. One way of thinking is to figure out that there are two dimensions to political success. One of them, of course, is to influence voters or elected officials. This is one facet. However, there are internal politics to the library, the university, the corporation and although they may be a smaller scale they are still important.

The understanding of politics is very important to raising money for the library. The purpose of the funds needs to be clearly established before the money is raised so that all stakeholders see the purpose of the activity and the library's needs for the money. There is often a correlation between the amount of money raised by a library to the degree of control that the library has over how it is spent. You seldom meet an employee or volunteer who is willing to work beyond their job description to raise money that just goes to the city.

It takes passion to raise money and people who support libraries tend to be more passionate about libraries than they are for general governments.

When one approaches the organization of a book covering a topic that provides thousands of sources and many, many concepts there must be a way to provide a familiar scenario for the reader that keeps the book in a flow. Some examples would be a map, a linear progression from little to big, and so on. Since many people are familiar with the organization of cookbooks one of them seemed to be a good analogy, but not just a *Betty Crocker Cookbook. The best ones are more than just listing the ingredients and steps for preparation.* They not only present recipes, but show menus for Christmas, etc., and provide helpful hints, what tools to use, how to organize your kitchen, when to do what, and show beautiful pictures of meals.

I haven't come up with a way to show pretty pictures of fundraising campaigns and activities, but maybe in my picture book version I can do that at least for building campaigns. The common element of many of the cookbooks are that they are prepared by signature chefs, rather than just cooks. The difference is these chefs know not only how to cook, they know how to run the business, give good customer service, and above all get great publicity. The same set of skills is important for a library leader to become successful in their field and their community.

While this book focuses on publicly funded libraries, it contains knowledge for other publicly funded education institution libraries and for other not-for-profit organizations with some relevant advice for corporate settings as well.

I

Getting Them Hungry (Putting Out the Bait)

For you to put out your bait, a part of the majority of the community, its leaders, and its current supporters must have the willingness to understand library needs for additional funds. Four areas create pressure for more funds: increased expectations by the stakeholders, loss of relevancy to former stakeholders, inflation (a factor that changes constantly), and investment funds for responding to the first three pressures. While change can make a library more efficient and effective so that in the long run there may be a reduction of strategic costs, implementing the needed changes almost always requires new monies or a rearrangement of priorities.

NEED FOR CHANGE

The need for change is documented in many recent studies. For example, a recent essay distributed by the American College and Research Libraries titled "Changing Roles of Academic and Research Libraries" provides a reasoned look at the future of academic libraries and the changing expectations of the academic community. As early as 2003, librarians in the United Kingdom developed a toolkit to help librarians make needed changes for their libraries. This shows that change in public libraries is a reality and costs money. Jeffrey Zaslow in the *Wall Street Journal* talks about how the younger generation sees the library as being less relevant to them than their grandparents do (Zaslow, 2007). A recent blog on American Library Association's (ALA) "ALA News" contends that even small town library directors spend a lot of time on fundraising (Laura, 2007; ALA Blog). In general, most people like libraries and will support them. Local and national polls show that libraries are among the most trusted and valued institutions. The primary reason that libraries have not received adequate funding is due to the fact that individuals and communities don't understand the choices for services of today and the cost of supporting them adequately.

COMMUNICATING WITH STAKEHOLDERS

This situation is often caused by a lack of communication from the library, negative economic conditions, or lack of leadership on the part of the librarian. The taxpayers and the employees must understand where the money comes from and why there is a need for more. The community must also believe that the current operation provides good value for what they pay. If they think the library is inefficient, overstaffed, or the employees are not managed well, it will be difficult to get the funding increased. If the librarians create a strong vision that is put forth in a good case statement that communicates well and creates increased commitment from the community, there will be increased resources.

A good children's library creates users, voters, and supporters. It may take some time for them to become voters but the children soon become eligible for voting. Public libraries need to place a priority on good children's librarians and excellent facilities for them. A good adult literacy program creates stakeholders who can be energized for library campaigns as well. Many of the participants in such a program have never been in a library or have never seen it as relevant to their lives. Once they have learned to read, their lives change dramatically and the library is in a good position to continue their learning. Often they feel willing to give back to the literacy program and the library. Be sure to give them that opportunity.

A good information access program including support for intellectual freedom, subsidized access, and advocacy on behalf of the users builds stakeholders. They become vested in the library and can be mobilized for support. A good strategic plan that includes mission, vision, strategic goals, benchmarks, and decision support information is the most important management tool possible. A good plan is one that is crafted with librarian values and ethics, involves the stakeholders, contains a clear and succinct mission and vision, presents straightforward goals and strategies that are measurable and achievable, and results in success.

This is where we create a lovely, informative, and tasty menu for our diners.

RAISING EXPECTATIONS

If you want to be the influence for change rather than just going with outside pressures such as technology, politics, or the economy, you need to be able to raise the expectations of the citizens and the community as to what the library can and should do. Experience shows that it is the most effective strategy for increasing resources. When most people are asked about what they want the library to be in the future, they tend to think back to their pleasant or productive experiences earlier in their life. It is difficult to get them to think about library futures in new terms. A really good starting point for setting the stage for the future is contained in an article from the Da Vinci Institute on the future of libraries. The executive director talks about the fact that communication systems are continually changing the way people access information, that all technology ends and will be replaced by something new, and that search technology will become increasingly more complicated which he sees as a positive sign for the continued need for librarians. We will take a more in-depth look at his points in Chapter 3 (Frey).

Another interesting approach to the creation of an image for the future of the library for stakeholders is in the Scandinavian Public Library Quarterly. In his article, Bruijnzeels provides seven possible scenarios for libraries in 2040. He is responsible for the development of a future strategy for Dutch public libraries and for the coordination of Information and Communication Technology (ICT) policy. His site also leads to a number of other excellent sites (Bruijnzeels). Many ideas about libraries in the future are presented by thinkers outside of librarianship and the United States. Some projected futures for libraries that indicate librarians are the ones that must change in order to preserve the future of the library.

At the International Federation of Library Associations (IFLA) 2007 conference, a paper presented by a speaker from the U.K. that stated that librarians need to abandon the traditional tenets of librarianship and need to become information professionals who will ally themselves with other fields in order to survive. The paper is very depressing since it implies that librarians would be extinct unless they change their ways (Broady-Preston, 2007). This is not new news since a similar view was presented in an article titled "The Panda Syndrome" over ten years ago. This article by two distinguished members of the U.S. Library and Information Science (LIS) faculty stated boldly that librarians like Pandas in China who are seeing their critical habitat disappearing due to community growth, must change their diet or have their turf protected by government (Van House and Sutton, 2000).

Survey information in the United States shows exactly the opposite in the United States and that librarians are thriving. The San Jose State University's (SJSU) School of Library and Information Science (SLIS) has over 2000 graduate students in their LIS program which is not only the largest group of graduate LIS students in any program in the world; it is the largest in history. One can't help wondering if the reason that libraries and librarians are in serious financial trouble in the U.K. is because the expectations of library stakeholders there are so low. The recent survey commissioned by ALA shows that while usage of libraries continues to remain strong and growing, it is in the area of the use of electronic sources where the largest growth is taking place. At the same time, the number of e-books in university libraries increased more than 68 percent in less than two years, i.e., from 2002 to 2004 (The State of America's Libraries, 2007). This shows that the libraries in the United States have been adapting to user needs and community goals quite well since it also shows that library visits per year to U.S. public libraries increased 61 percent between 1994 and 2004. There is more detail about their view in Chapter 2 in the discussion of dysfunctional myths.

The IFLA Congress was full of examples of where librarians have made a difference in their communities and their nations. It was announced at the IFLA Congress that 1 billion rand had been recently appropriated from the federal government for libraries in that country. A local South African newspaper headlined it as "Bookies Get a Billion" (Mail and Guardian Online, 2007). Even when converted to U.S. dollars, which comes to about $139,996,978, it is a lot of money. The stated purpose of the money is to get books into libraries and to create a new tradition of reading, which has not been valued by many of the citizens of South Africa. They also received a UNESCO grant in 2006 to train thirty public library workers.

A librarian from the Jamaican National Library gave an interesting program at IFLA on the progress they are making in providing library services to remote areas. They have a number of successful partnerships including one with Kentucky Fried Chicken to fund a reading center called "Chicky Reads."

The Sarawak State Library in Malaysia made presentations on the tremendous progress in library development in their country. The telephone company is required to fund networking in the communities and since much of Malaysia has no outside source of electricity, the minister of energy has a mandate to fund local solutions for lack of electrical infrastructure with alternate sources such as generators. They also use satellites for connecting to remote sites. They are eagerly looking forward to the delivery of their first BoatMobile. Their goal is to train 735,000 people on information literacy by the end of 2008. As part of their effort to stimulate the citizens to get online university admission, applicants must fill out the form online. They are using the library and its new technology to improve the knowledge of citizens about Information Literacy as measured by the Knowledge Index and to improve the quality of life of inhabitants (Bolhassan, 2007).

SURVEYING YOUR COMMUNITY

As professionals we should be surveying the landscapes constantly, assessing how the library in the future can optimize its value to the community, and how you can get there. You can't do this alone, but you are the one with that responsibility. If you are to be successful in creating a shared vision for the future, you must enlist and accept the views of those members of the community who are willing to participate, and provide the leadership to ensure the process moves forward.

A major challenge is getting the public to think about the library in terms that are cogent with the future, not the nostalgic past. In the 1970s, Pikes Peak Library District (PPLD) used the emerging Public Library Planning Process developed at ALA to help build the vision of the future of the library for the PPLD. It was a major project requiring nearly two years and significant expenditure of staff and community members' time for completion. It included formal surveys, many community meetings, and focus groups to gather the wishes of the community about the library and its services.

While the results didn't find any major breakthroughs in creating the vision of the future, it was clear that the process brought in many new stakeholders and increased the commitment of those already on board. In retroflection, what was missing was the ability of the average person to project functions of the library into the future other than what they liked from their past or present services of the library. Since this was very early in the development of the computers and online networking (the minicomputer was just appearing, the microcomputer was on the horizon, and the Internet wasn't even on the radar screen of the average person) there were very few citizens who foresaw the huge impact of the new technology.

Colorado Springs did have a lot of people involved in high technology because of the military installations and early high technology companies located there, so citizens were more aware than most communities. Even with that kind of community there were few forward thinking responses generated out of the planning effort. We did find that the process worked well for establishing communication and wide-ranging networks among the community members, their organizations, and the library. The knowledge gained did show that most people feel the library is beneficial to the community and to themselves.

It was obvious that the approach had to be changed and that options needed to be developed for the community to respond to. A local community research nonprofit firm agreed to do a statistically valid survey of the population based on giving them options. In that survey, people were asked to respond to questions that related to a new future for the library. The survey is reported in the University of Illinois Clinic Proceedings for 1983 (Dowlin and Magrath, 1983). In order to deal with the future it was necessary to rephrase the mission of the library in much broader terms than the traditional library. In summary, it asked the individual if they felt that the first role of PPLD should include a community published resource center. It was explained that this meant providing the traditional functions of librarianship, which are often stated as the collection, preservation, organization, and distribution of books and other printed materials (or their facsimiles such as microform).

The second role was to serve as a community information center which meant providing current and forward-looking information access such as community events data bases, community information resources data bases, and a community focal point for access to all kinds of information. The third role was to serve as a community communication center which meant that the library would provide programming and information through any current technology available such as cable television programs, programs in library facilities, and remote online access to library resources.

The last question was to ascertain if the citizens felt that PPLD was a good investment of the tax dollars in the community. This was to determine their current view of the management and operation of the current library. This was an important indicator of real and potential support for the library. The results showed that the community was amenable to the goals presented and that the effort to receive 50 percent plus one vote was definitely feasible. Only a simple majority of the votes in a funding referendum for the PPLD was required. Armed with this information, PPLD was able to go to the government over-sight agencies, which included the state legislature (to raise the statutory mill levy limit) and then to the voters to get the mill levy increased (two times). The same process had to be replicated to get the bonds for a new regional library approved.

These lessons learned led to a different approach in San Francisco. The starting point was a vision for the library that grew out of hiring a new city librarian. A citizen attitude survey in 1998 provided data for the expansion of the vision and suggested strategies to use to increase support for the library (Rund and O'Donnell, 1998). It was funded by the California State Library and was conducted by a political polling company. A simple but clear view of a positive future for the library by the community emerged. The people surveyed responded to specific components for a future library developed from the experience at PPLD and the respondents could express their opinions on them. The survey gave a very strong clue as to how much they would pay for a new library. Since personal computing and networking was just evolving, few citizens had thought of the potential that these new technologies had for libraries but a surprisingly large number of respondents agreed that this technology was very important to the library of the future. The survey reinforced previous experience and its impact in getting the ball rolling was very important.

It was a major breakthrough in library surveys to find out general parameters for the level of cost that the public would support. In general, it demonstrated that the cost of the library improvement programs was not the primary issue for the community. The three most valued priorities (each scored over 80 percent in favor) were state of the art technology, a world-class library, and an outstanding children's center. The children's center was a surprise since the demographic data for the city showed that only 16 percent of the population was children. It turns out that in San Francisco even people who do not have children thought that children's library service is very important. This research played a major role in getting the support of the elected and appointed officials and then overwhelming approval by the voters for a bond issue for a new main library, branch renovation, and a long-term dedicated budget for the library. This trend has continued in San Francisco. The voters have approved two more bond issues for branch library improvements and are considering another one. They also recently approved a fifteen-year extension of the dedicated revenue imitative passed almost fifteen years ago.

IDENTIFYING STAKEHOLDERS AND LINKING COMMUNICATIONS

It is important to put in place a system for identifying stakeholders and linking together the communications process to communicate with them regularly. We know that the public generally likes libraries and will support their funding if they regard the library as an efficient and effective public service that meets their needs (OCLC, 2005). But, we must pay attention to changes in attitudes and expectations that are changing very rapidly. For example, while the card catalog may seem nostalgic, even valuable to some people, virtually all research studies show that they are not only costly and inaccurate, but the public today generally feel that they are a waste of time. This attitude is authenticated by a recent OCLC survey. It found that 90 percent of people surveyed used search engines for finding information, that less than 1 percent used OPACS, and 80 percent were satisfied with results of search engine (OCLC, 2005). The attitude change in the public toward library automation and networking has shifted 180 degrees from the 1970s when pioneering was taking place in those areas. Any librarian advocating the use of computers in libraries in the 1970s had to spend time justifying the library even having a computer. Now it is almost impossible to find a library that doesn't have a computer or uses a networked operation on a computer somewhere.

While there are different routes to take to increase the public's support and willingness to increase the resources for programs, services, and facilities of a library, the most successful strategy is to raise the expectations in the people and leaders in the community. Some people are aware of what other libraries are doing but you need to ensure that all members in the community are presented with information and knowledge that raises their expectations for their own library. Programs in the library, electronic communication channels, and networking with other libraries can inform the public. It is a good idea to link the Web sites of libraries with outstanding Web sites and online services into your Web site so that your stakeholders can see what the possibilities are. Check out the Web site of Farkas to see her list of the honor role of library Web sites (Farkas, Website Design).

In showing the public the services of other libraries and information organizations, educating them on the possibilities, and creating a strategic development program, you should take the leadership in moving the library forward. All of this is only the first step in a long-term process. It is important prior to actually starting the fundraising campaigns or initiatives to check around the library for threats to your success that may jump up and bite you. Part of the reason for this book is to alert those of you engaged in strategic fundraising of ghosts from the past of your library that may come forward to derail your development program. It is so easy for people who do not support the library or the goals of the library's leadership to drag red herrings across the path of the campaign. They may or may not derail the campaign but they can eat up an inordinate amount of resources that could be used for something else.

2

Cleaning Out the Kitchen

Before we start at getting the tools, the other cooks, the cookbooks, and the recipes, we need to clean out the kitchen that we have. It is rare, at least in the library world, that one gets a totally new kitchen. While a librarian may dream about having the opportunity to create a totally new public library system which would allow them to do everything from scratch or imported from someplace else, this is not likely to happen. While you would like to leave behind historic baggage, attitudes, and barriers, you must acknowledge them and move ahead. Most library directors come into libraries as a replacement for someone else who may have been the director for many years. Even those who had done wonderful jobs and were well respected in their circles may have allowed the library to become static or in a rut. So, if you are new in the library, or have a new mandate to raise money, you should consider cleaning house, remembering that change does cause some level of chaos.

If you arrive at a library where staff has not seemed to recognize their need to be involved or supportive of obtaining funding beyond what they are allocated by their funding bodies, you may need to make some changes, and you may also consider ways to clean house. This is essential if you want your library to keep its relevance in your community. We can approach the topic by looking at the myths that have to be dealt with, getting rid of the baggage, and then implementing programs that will move you into politics and fundraising.

MINIMIZING DYSFUNCTIONAL MYTHS

Myths often create barriers to success, and there are a number of myths that still persist in the library community about the library staff, budget and collections, and the role of the librarian in politics and fundraising. We need to consider them early in our thinking. It is important to know how to understand and maneuver those issues that the myth brings forth so that those who believe in the myths can't create barriers to your funding efforts.

Let's start with the big ones about libraries that include librarians aren't needed anymore now that we have computers, or the Internet can replace the librarian. If you want ammunition to counter the people who believe the myth that technology (in any of its variants) will replace a library go to http://www.degreetutor.com/library/adult-continued-education/librarians-needed for thirty-three reasons why libraries will persist.

A somewhat lesser, but prevalent one is that anyone can run a library. The public often has much confusion about who does what in a library and what of education and experience it takes for the different jobs. Often a patron approaching the circulation desk or seeing someone shelving books will think this is a professional librarian when it is a library technician. They may be very good at their job and are happy to help the customer; they may not have the training or knowledge to meet the user's needs. It is very difficult to know what you don't know.

Even more difficult to overcome is the belief that volunteers can take the place of personnel for the service and operation of the library. Because staff is always the major cost in the library budget, it is a myth that must be countered with careful explanations of the various tasks in the library and the qualifications necessary or those tasks to be completed. While slow, the staffing patterns and competencies of the different jobs in a library are being reassessed and modified to reflect current needs and practice. Joan Frye Williams, a library and information technology consultant, often points out that libraries are one of the few organizations that put their most educated and professional persons on the front desk. This situation requires the library to hire employees who have the education, skills, and pay level to handle many routine or procedural questions that can be answered by people with different skill sets and often at less cost. Many different kinds of tasks need to be done in today's libraries that require people with a variety of skills. This is especially true for fundraising.

People with skills such as researching donors, managing a capital campaign, organizing functions and events can truly expand the abilities of the organization. These people need not be expected to have the same education as librarians in the values, ethics, commitment to service, and skills that the librarians have. They may have been hired for their professional skill set which is different from the librarians'. In this case, it is the organization's responsibility to orient them to these aspects of the library.

Another myth is that a library can be operated from monies raised by book sales and other public events. Many public libraries were started by volunteers or community organizations and only later could count on public funding. Even today the evolution of some libraries from the historical pattern to the modern funding base for public libraries continues. The organization and funding for libraries in areas of Massachusetts is very complicated with the different regional approaches, towns, cities, counties, and boroughs.

A really dysfunctional myth is that many librarians feel that they didn't become librarians to become managers and certainly not managers who had to find ways to raise funds outside their allocated budget. That may have been true at one time. It was possible to get a job cataloging, or working on the reference desk where you weren't expected to manage in the traditional sense. Very few jobs are left in libraries that don't require management of something or someone. With the increasing levels of librarians' salaries, the parent governments are expecting librarians will be used at supervisory levels or higher with nondegreed staff to manage the desks and provide much of the customer support. In addition, many of the traditional tasks performed in a library have become automated, outsourced, or networked, thus requiring fewer librarians in those tasks. A librarian who has the motivation, education, and training can be very effective managing people with very specific skills and can take the lead in fundraising for their institutions.

Some people take the historic view of a library and its collections believing that a library must keep every book. What this means is that even when the shelves are full of books, it is difficult to convince them that the collection needs additional materials even though what is filling those spaces are books that no one has read in years if not decades. To the casual viewer, the library has more than enough books. This group of myths point out the need for the library to have a clear, community-based mission, vision, and goals position relative to their collections.

Other myths add to confusion on the part of all the stakeholders including some librarians. For example, librarians should not be involved in politics. Perhaps it has to do with how "involved in politics" is defined.

A small town city council member who went on to become a state senator and a federal judge told me early in my career that "to be successful as a library director you must be involved in politics but you needed to be apolitical, not nonpolitical." While library directors must be careful about being partisan or candidate specific about issues or candidates, they must be involved and understand what is happening. Librarians who are knowledgeable about the political process will succeed in expanding and enhancing the library they lead.

Another myth is that all politics are local. This statement is an outmoded concept in today's networked, real time, global environment. It is still true that if you are dealing primarily with totally local issues that the focus should be on the local politics. That is where it all starts. However, it is less and less clear about which politics are local, state, national, and even international. This why the profession needs to have a multiple-level focus with state-level professional associations, national-level associations, and even international associations with their missions of advancing the profession and libraries. Librarians must be actively involved in as many as possible. Some people believe that all politicians are alike. Not true. Many wonderful elected and appointed officials are dedicated to doing the best possible job in their offices. When you meet them, treasure them and keep them involved as stakeholders. They will help you overcome the distaste of meeting and dealing with officials that are self-serving, unethical, immoral, and just plain slimy.

Some view politics as dramatic and quickly changing which is usually another myth. Politics are most often fragmented, incremental, and usually sequential. One of the huge obstacles for many librarians is the long lead times required for public funding. Most cities require at least one year of lead time before approving annual budgets and often two or more. One of the worst examples is the budget cycle for the Washington, D.C. Public Library. Any significant change in budget took at least seven years. It had to go through not only all of the city processes but also the federal appropriations and expenditure cycles. Success for libraries with politics requires planning ahead, focus on task, and commitment to the end goal.

In the government world it is usually the practice to award a contract or purchase a service from the lowest bidder without appropriate consideration for the potential for fraud or even ineptness on the part of the vendor. While being thrifty is usually viewed as a virtue and it is important that the library be seen as an institution that is prudent in expenditures, there are situations where cheapest is not the best. Sometimes the priority should be the net difference, not how much an item costs. In simpler terms, if an item costs $1,000 and provides $5,000 worth of benefit it is better to spend the $1,000 if the $500 one returns only $2,000 worth of benefit.

A vivid example of this is with the San Francisco Public Library's (SFPL) new main library (NML) and the process in purchasing and installing the book transport system within the NML. Since the system was purchased under the bond funds, it was subject to the procedures that the city uses for purchases under the general contract. The system that was selected was under-engineered, poorly installed, and is practically a waste of time and money. The supplier had no experience in the design and installation of a book distribution system in a library.

On the other hand, since the furniture and building space enhancements were purchased by the foundation, an entirely different process was used. The emphasis was on design, functionality, and durability. Cost was not the primary consideration. The lesson learned is that sometimes excellence is expensive but the net difference makes it worth it. The reader's tables and chairs were very expensive but not only are they attractive they can be expected to last for many years due to the testing by the Princeton University materials testing program for durability.

The point here is that there is a myth that governments either overspend based on erroneous procurement practices or buy shoddy and cheap. Most people do feel that government-provided service is more often than not mediocre and if the opportunity for excellence can be presented, they are more apt to provide additional funding from the private sector. It takes money to make money; and, if you use public funding to provide the basic services wisely, you are more likely to get private support to go beyond the basic services. In this way you can leverage public funding to increase nongovernment funding. The nongovernment funding can also be used to sell the stakeholders on the need for additional government funding.

One of the biggest myths to making a change for the better in a library's operation or services is that the library doesn't have the money. That is a real cop-out since the reason that they don't have the money is that they don't have the talent and leadership to get the job done. Sometimes the talent is just the ability to realize that you need to find better talent to support you. If you have talented people who are committed to the library, provide the leadership for a strategic development program, and spend the time to get it accomplished, you can succeed. This is perhaps the most crippling myth that impedes library advancement. Lack of funds does not have to be a barrier to success. With time, talent, commitment, and a capacity to create knowledgeable stakeholders, any goal that is based on rational arguments and emotional appeal can be reached.

Another myth is that libraries can't compete with museums and other cultural institutions for big bucks. This may be true in some situations especially in larger cities with the long established entities. Museums have been raising significant funds for a long time and have recruited many of the major people who have the money and the tradition of philanthropy in the community. On the other hand the public library is the most populist institution in the community. Everyone can become passionate about the library and will give what they can when they know what the possibilities are when the money is there.

One possibility is to get invited to join a social group of the directors of major cultural institutions. In this situation, a director has the opportunity for sharing their expertise and in learning from the others. The Class of 87 in San Francisco brought together the president of the San Francisco Public Broadcasting Station (KQED), the president of the Board for the San Francisco Ballet, the director of the San Francisco Opera, the director of the Museum of Modern Art, the director of the Fine Arts Museum, the director of the Asian Art Museum, and the city librarian. While the members shared ideas and enthusiasm for the cultural scene in San Francisco, we were careful to not poach on another's major donors. These types of organizations usually have a long history of fundraising and can provide the library director insight into their worlds. It also expands the library's view relative to being a major cultural organization as well. Some crossover of supporters and donors exists, and many are willing to support more than one cause. The opportunity to rub shoulders with the supporters of the other cultural organizations at other social and professional events is critical. Library staff may be able to provide technical support in some areas to the other cultural institutions. Belonging to this type of group gives the library credibility in the philanthropic circles.

Now that we have looked at some of the myths that seem to create barriers to what we need to do, let's look at fundamentals that we need to observe while we are cleaning out the kitchen. First, how do we know what to toss and what to keep in our kitchen and how do we explain what we are doing to our community? Let's begin with the first fundamental truth.

The library director needs to understand the big picture. While it is much easier to find a librarian who is detail orientated than it is to find one who gets the big picture, at the upper levels of the organization everyone must understand the big picture. Top-level funding successes require strategic and systemic thinkers and doers. They must not only need to be able to manage, but lead. A good leader needs to know when leadership is called for and when management skills are required. A good leader also needs to recognize when the skill or motivation to be a good manager is missing, and someone should be hired to run the organization on a day-to-day basis.

A number of people in the 1990s felt that more money should be spent on books or staff for the NML, and not technology. This is very naïve in the twenty-first century. The public seldom realizes that two-thirds of the library budget is taken up with staff cost, and it is critical to use technology to lower those costs. The efficiency of libraries in the circulation of materials and maintaining inventory control has increased tremendously with the implementation of automation; and, while there is a cost for the automation, the increase in worker productivity through automation is one of the reasons that the inflation rate is low today.

We need to decide which to throw out and which to keep. In order to make those decisions we need to have a tool or method for evaluating their value.

ASSESSING EFFECTIVENESS AND EFFICIENCY

In Marine Corps training, one of the exercises to ensure that the troops are taking care of their equipment, clothing, and area for which they are responsible is called a Junk on the Bunk Inspection. Put everything out for inspection and organize it as shown in the *Marine Corps Handbook*. While it isn't possible to put every program in a library through such an exercise every year, the library should have an ongoing process for the evaluation of the efficiency and effectiveness of all of the programs and services.

While many definitions of effectiveness and efficiency exist, a common agreement is that efficiency is based on the ratio of inputs to outputs, services, or assets. Money is the most common denominator. Efficiency was the dimension most often researched and reported about for libraries in the 1960s and 1970s. If you agree on the measurements, it becomes relatively mathematical to measure efficiency. If the number of books circulated goes up and the cost remains the same, the library is more efficient in that dimension. If the function remains static but the cost goes down, that is also an increase in efficiency. The super hope is that the function goes up and the cost comes down. Unfortunately, efficiency is more easily measured in the corporate sector where the bottom line is usually financial profit.

Effectiveness is defined as the ability of any organization to meet their mission, vision, and goals. This is also true of a library. Defining and measuring effectiveness is much more complicated than defining or measuring efficiency. This applies whether the goals are financial, service oriented, or political. The measurement becomes tricky because of the question of who supplies the goals and the fact that there may be perceptual goals as well as physical ones. In the public sector, most of the time the perception of goal attainment is just as important as the reality. What the community thinks of the library is just as important or maybe more important than how many people use their libraries. Effectiveness measurement methodologies have been recently developed for libraries. For example, the Balanced Scorecard Methodology has gained considerable implementation (Matthews, 2007).

To determine efficiency and effectiveness, it is critical to create measures of success and time periods for continual evaluation. This brings a certain discipline to the organization. The measurements used to determine success need to be reevaluated for their significance or even relevance. In the distant past, the number of books circulated and owned and the number of reference question answered were the primary measurements for libraries. While people are still asking questions at the service desks today, most current evidence shows that the number of questions is getting fewer in number. The most significant factor in this equation is the changing natures of the questions. In the 1960s, a reference question was deemed to be counted when the librarian referred a user to a print publication that would provide information to answer the user's needs. In the 1970, in designing the first library Decision Support System, The Pike's Peak Library District (PPLD) broke down the different components related to public service. We found that the traditional measurements were inadequate to measure the activities, and thus the goal attainment of the library (Dowlin and Magrath, 1983). Today, the successful library is much more complex. The statistics collected now include visits to the facilities, electronic transactions, and other functions that are much more relevant in measuring effectiveness and efficiency.

Since any increases in the budget often have elections by the electorate, their perceptions become a very important part of the process. One of the real positive developments in libraries is the fact that there are many people who don't use the library, yet feel that the library is important to the community. For funding purposes the question isn't how many people use the library, it is how many people think that the library is useful, and good value.

Today there is much more information for planning for libraries. Sources of measurement statistics for all public libraries from Hennen's American Public Library Ratings Index, the American Library Association, and other sources are a good starting point. Tom Hennen should be commended for his work in advancing the state of the art of measurement of library services (Hennen, 2001). Linda Ferguson prepared a Webography on library statistics and performance measure that is a bit outdated but still useful as pointers (Ferguson). In Chapter 7, the methodology used in the SFPL library elections to convince the public of the need for an NML will be discussed.

GETTING RID OF THE BAGGAGE

While the library's programs and operations should be assessed continuously and formalized on a regular basis it is important to fundraising that the community feels that the library is well managed and the existing budget is well spent. Some time should be spent on becoming more efficient and effective as a part of the early planning phases.

It would be ideal if you had the time and the resources to go through the library program by program and service by service and assess the efficiency and effectiveness of all of them. This was the basis for some of the budget systems in the 1970s and 1980s such as Zero Based Budgeting or Planned Program Budgeting. The methodology for those were applied in various city, state, and even federal programs and generally collapsed under the weight of management and administration of the program. The other fallacy of these programs was that, in the time it took to get them implemented, the mayor or president had served out their term and the successor wasn't interested in the program. The process of reaching agreement in the goals and measurements was a political process which usually meant that it took a long time to reach agreement.

MINIMIZING THE NEGATIVE RUMOR MILL

It seems like every library has a rumor mill where even simple events can blossom into huge issues with the stakeholders in the library. This author used the opportunity during the coursework for a Master's in Public Administration degree to search for a way to turn a negative rumor mill into a positive communication tool. The research did not come up with a sure-fire tool to counter the rumor but there were indications that a healthy, accurate, and timely communications system could dispel some of the rumors that seem to go around. In libraries that have constant change of political leadership and in the library, it is common that the loyalty of the staff tends to migrate to their friends and long-term colleagues as opposed to the institution, the political leaders, and often the library leaders. This is a very difficult culture to change and requires an excellent educational system for the staff.

The research suggested that open communication with all possible stakeholders creates a climate for positive stories. Having a strong online communication program provides an unparalleled opportunity for direct communications to the user that can focus on the user's concerns yet broadcast the responses so that everyone sees them. A number of librarians dedicate a bulletin board in the library to questions asked by people, and the posted responses allowed everyone to see the questions and the answers. In today's world, the blog seems to be an excellent answer. Check out the one at the Ann Arbor, Michigan District Library which has incorporated blogs seamlessly into its Web site (www.aadl.org).

One of the most basic steps for clear communication is having documented policies and procedures that are available to everyone. This is an excellent function for your Web site.

CLARIFY AND CODIFY POLICIES, PROCEDURES, FEEDBACK, AND CONTROL SYSTEM

In order to have a comprehensive education and training program for the staff it is necessary to document procedures, policy, and service norms. They need to be written down and adopted by the appropriate person or persons. A good rule of management is to follow the practice that the body that adopted the procedure or policy should have the authority to do so, and they should be the ones to modify or delete a policy. The codification of procedures and policies in a large, historic library can be very time consuming but it is important that all stakeholders know what they are and when any change takes place. A system needs to be in place for the management of the communication and documentation of policies and procedures. The Couberg Public Library has an excellent Web site (http://www.Couberg.lib.on.ca). It has a clear presentation of the policies of the library.

EDUCATE AND INFORM THE STAFF

While it is important that the staff understand the mission, vision, and goals of the library and be able to present these to the other stakeholders anytime, this becomes critical during a time for a fund drive or referendum on the library. The staff working with the public has the opportunity working with the public and the responsibility to the organization to help create satisfied stakeholders, and one needs satisfied stakeholders to be in favor of new funding projects. A good approach is to train the staff in good customer-relations skills. Several ways to do this include a good communications system for the staff, work to help them see a bigger picture, and to make sure staff development is funded.

Many tools can be used to create robust and trusted online communications systems for the staff. These can be used to keep them updated and to encourage them to support the mission and goals of the library. The tools that the libraries implement to create and communicate with stakeholders can easily be applied to the internal staff communications network. The author knows of at least one library that started their staff meetings with a recitation of the mission statement. While this sounds extreme to library culture, it seemed to be an effective way to build the staff team. The mission, vision, and strategic goals should be part of the orientation of all new staff members and should be reinforced regularly with the rest of the staff. It is critical that the staff communications system be inclusive, up–to-date, and it evolves with the changes that take place in the organization and services. It needs to be approached as a part of the strategic system.

One of the most effective ways to expand the horizons of the staff members is to have exchange programs with other libraries. Staff from one library can go to another for a while and staff from that library can come to yours. At PPLD, staff was regularly exchanged with other libraries, but probably staff members who were there most remember their experience when they went to the Bibliotheque du Public Information at the Pompidou Center in Paris. While such unusual exchanges may not be possible, exchanging with the next town over will allow staff to experience another situation and to share ideas and to bring good ideas back to their library.

Providing educational opportunities for the staff at SFPL was challenging to say the least. Getting funds in the regular budget was virtually impossible; and, if it wasn't for the Friends of the Library support, we would have had little attendance at workshops and conferences. It is strange that cities and libraries spend thousands of dollars every year maintaining their copy machines, computers, and other equipment, but the amount of money spent on updating staff is nominal at best.

Once we have done the house cleaning then we are ready for bringing in the new tools and equipment that we need to get the development program underway.

3

Organizing the Kitchen (Strategic Thinking)

It's time to start organizing our kitchen with strategic thinking as our guide. It is often difficult to prioritize these efforts because one does not necessarily follow the other. You are never in total control of your timing or the flow of resources to accomplish each task and so it is important to stay focused but flexible on the details. In our approach, we will group the activities into four major groups:

1. Build your personal knowledge and skills
2. Identify your community
3. Identify your barriers
4. Get your vision out to the public

Each one of these and the subsets under them should be on your agenda somewhere and while your attention may focus on one or a few at a time, you keep all of them on your list and in your thinking.

PERSONAL KNOWLEDGE AND SKILLS DEVELOPMENT

The successful library leader will know more about the big picture and will have skills specific to their responsibility. The ability to form the larger picture and communicate this scenario to others is unique from the abilities needed at the nonstrategic level of responsibility. One the other hand it isn't possible for any one person to have mastered all of the skills and to know everything that you need to know to be a library leader. To do all of the tasks needed for a major development project may require knowledge of architecture, technology, fundraising, putting on social events, and many other tasks not taught in library schools. You should however, be on a constant quest for improvement for yourself and for your staff. If you don't have the time to learn, it is possible to compensate for knowledge that you lack by having people on your team who have that skill. When we get into specific types of activities for development of a large library, you will find that you will need to be skillful in areas for which you are often not personally prepared.

A successful leader for a strategic development program needs the ability to continue to learn, to spot talent, to enlist talent to your pool of supporters, and to leverage all the resources. Most of these skills aren't just specific to libraries but they are certainly important to the leaders in libraries. They start with developing your own vision, values, mission, and even dreams for the library. Ensuring that you can cover some basic leadership skills such as listening, learning to observe dynamics in meetings, learning to keep learning, learning to educate others, and making effective presentations including giving testimony in formal hearings. It is a huge challenge to master all of them since they range from financial management, to marketing, and to inspiring stakeholders. Above all, a library leader must be clear on what their job is and their goals in order to be successful.

Develop Your Own Vision, Values, Mission, and Even Dreams for the Library

Think of vision building as cyclical. Start with yourself and create your vision for the library. Your vision needs to include a wide variety of views, be strategic, and long-term. You will be sharing it first with your immediate support team so they can help shape it and feel ownership of the shared vision. Then you should imbed it into the training and communication program for all employees and then move it out to a wider circle of stakeholders. Therefore, it must be carefully crafted, and you must be certain it has all the elements that are essential.

You will take it to your support groups such as the Friends of the Library (FOL) and the Library Foundation. You will be constantly touching base with your stakeholders and seeking their input and support. You will be the sales person for the shared vision. Vision building includes assessing stakeholders and organizing them into groups for communication and support purposes, building community within the stakeholders, establishing the library's brand and credibility. Articulate and polish your vision, but don't trap yourself into the position that your vision is absolute and uncaring about the other stakeholder's visions. Once you have polished and tested your vision it is time to use it for guiding the strategic plan development and implementation.

DO YOUR HOMEWORK

Build Your Case Statement

The case statement should include a clear and succinct mission statement. A really good focus for a mission statement is on the stakeholders. A mission is best defined from a customer's point of view. Rather than simply describing your products and services, describe the benefits or capability your customers acquire as a result of interacting with you. A vision statement should be included which presents the image of where the library wants to be in the future. It should be a clear statement of community needs that is based on research and polls; and for development purposes, the need for nongovernmental funding to ensure the success of the library should be articulated. The strategic goals are the steps you must accomplish in order to meet your mission and vision. One of the strategic goals must be to obtain adequate funding to meet the mission and the vision.

The concept that the nonpublic money is needed for excellence is a good strategy. Most people think that the government should provide the money for basic operations. They may contribute for specific programs that they want, but they are generally reluctant to provide basic program support money as individuals or groups. You will need to include comparisons with other libraries to make your case for additional funding. You will need to communicate the need to the current stakeholders (the users, the elected officials, and others who generally support the library). If it is an issue for the voters then you need to convince the governing body of the need to put it on the ballot.

The Public Library Association and the National Center for Educational Statistics are good sources for research and useful data for building your case. In working through them, make the case by creating a table of parameters that would apply to your library and to similar libraries. Some of the criteria are size of library, historic nature of the main library, number of branches, numbers of books, circulation statistics and so on. If you create a spreadsheet using those criteria, you will find matching libraries in North America. Rank those libraries by size of book collections, building space, and other factors and show where your library falls. A list can be created that shows a comparison among the funding levels and resources of the libraries

The bottom line of all this strategy is once the data is collected and presented, you can create a Bumper Sticker Slogan. Elected officials and lukewarm supporters who are geographically chauvinistic will buy into the message.

What it showed for San Francisco Public Library (SFPL) was that it ranked number ten on the list of eleven. The top libraries in the chart were all in Ohio which was a surprise to most people in San Francisco. The top library on the list was the Cleveland Public Library who had almost four times as many books in their main library and was providing a host of excellent services. The Bumper Sticker Slogan was "San Franciscans deserved a library at least as good as the one in Cleveland."

While it is controversial, the data and the rankings of public libraries in the United States in the Hennen's American Public Library Ratings index provide an excellent benchmark for comparison of your library with other public libraries (Hennen, 2001). Often those librarians who receive high rankings for their libraries place that fact on their Web page and use it for publicity. It is certainly something to be proud of for those who rank high and something to shoot for those who don't make the list. The Pike's Peak Library District made the top ten in the last go around of rankings, a stage set years ago when the mill levy was increased after an excellent public relations program was established; however, the credit goes to the existing staff, the Board of Trustees, and the community. It would be interesting to build a rubric for moving a library up the list.

Learn to Observe and Chart Group Dynamics in Meetings

While watching political or government meetings, it is a good exercise to chart who talks to whom, who seems to be running the meeting, where the power is, and who drives the agenda and decisions. Sometimes they are not officials that have the titles. Many assistants, consultants, financial supporters, and others have influence, but they are not necessarily participating in what is going on in the meeting. The process that you would use is called a group communications audit. When you are sitting in meetings and the topic is peripheral to what you are there for, you should start observing who talks to whom, when they talk, and what their motives are. Make at least a mental diagram of the communication flow in the meeting. This can often help you identify who is actually in control of the meeting, who has the power, and who are the ones that you should cultivate. Often the real power isn't in the hand of the appointed or elected leader of the group.

Learn to Learn

As we go about our lives, we should always be involved in learning. We must keep that curiosity alive and explore and learn new ideas, skills, and techniques. You should take your opportunities to learn all of the time. You will be rewarded for doing so. It allows you to expand not only your horizons but to expand the horizons of those around you. You want to get the best out of people in the organization. Your staff will recognize your interest in learning new ideas and they will be willing to feed you information as they run across it. This provides a great network for everyone's learning growth. State, regional, and national library associations provide numerous learning opportunities. Take opportunities to read professional literature, attend conferences and workshops, and network with colleagues so that you are aware of what other libraries are doing.

New opportunities can increase the success in the library in meeting its vision and goals. Some of these opportunities may not be all that obvious. Missed opportunities are sad but they should be treated as a lesson learned and the library moves on.

The greatest attribute is to learn to listen to others. Many politicians tune out what their supporters and communities are saying to them. Perhaps it is because of the concentration of information that flows from the news media or opinion polls. However, not listening to your supporters and communities directly can get a library director in trouble.

Learn to Educate Others

While teaching and preaching are well known skills in management circles there is a lesser known skill called normative reeducation. It was explained in a book titled the *Cybernetic Theory of Decision* (Steinbruner, 1974). While the book is somewhat dated, it contained some seminal concepts for influencing or managing people and organizations. Steinbruner argues that it is time to take a new theoretical perspective on government decision-making processes. He urges us to take theory from a number of fields such as information theory and behavioral psychology. While he used the issue of sharing nuclear weapons among the NATO allies as an illustration of his theory, this was quite different from the situation to which this author was applying the knowledge.

You will be trying to influence elected and appointed officials to support the library. Many of them seemed indifferent and a few may be downright hostile. Loosely applying the concepts put forth by Steinbruner proved to be very successful when creating political stakeholders from elected officials. With a passing knowledge of applied psychology, one begins to realize that these folks weren't irrational; in fact they were perfectly rational. You just need to find out what their goals were. You may find groupings of behavior.

Easy officials to influence are those who have just never used the library and didn't see any need to do so. If these persons are given the opportunity to learn that the library either has services that would be useful to them or that people they listened too valued the library, they could be convinced to support the library. The next level is the ones that took months or even years to realize that library services can meet their personal or political needs. It is always effective to demonstrate to officials that the library has access to information that they need. This makes it clear that there are many opportunities for people to learn what they need to know.

The third type of officials is a larger challenge. They are not interested in the library's needs for funding, don't use the library themselves, and think that higher education isn't particularly important to one's career. If none of the communications or education influences them, then you must resort to the more drastic strategy. You either get enough voters to get them out of office or make them think that you could. As you become more and more successful in your development programs, the easier it becomes to convince all three levels. It is usually the first few that are the hardest.

Learn to Present

When you are invited to speak to a group you should have a repertoire of different speeches based on the type of the group and the length of time they want you to speak. Often the group will have something in mind when they decide to call you. Be sure to do your homework so that you can answer questions as well. Learn how to handle the different styles of the questioners. Some folks are truly after information and some of them like to hear themselves talk or have an agenda that is different than yours. Practice, practice, practice!

It is helpful to prepare and practice the different styles. Whether you are presenting short pithy messages identified as Bumper Sticker Communication, testifying in hearings, or making formal presentations to an audience, each is different. Prepare your audio/visual support tools. While PowerPoint presentations are still popular, the trend is now to keep them short, to the point, and without a lot of visual distractions. And remember, the message that you are presenting is really about them, not you. What is in it for them?

One excellent way to learn is to watch others who are successful and learn from them. Notice how they engage the audience and how the audience reacts. Separate the demagogs from the knowledgeable, honest leaders in your causes. When you do present, solicit feedback. You can get a sense of the audience's perceptions if you ask them if what you just said makes sense. If they say no, or you can see it in their eyes that they appear lost, restate your point.

A good speaker will get the audience engaged in the presentation. Build on their affirmative body language. Watch their eyes. In a large presentation setting, pick out individuals throughout the audience. Have one in the front, on the left, on the right, in the back, and perhaps others. As you speak, move your view from one to another so that they feel personally engaged. If you are speaking to a group with a different cultural background, be sensitive to their listening or participation styles. In some cultures an audience may be enjoying the presentation very much but their style is to avoid eye contact with the speaker.

Stick to the time allocated to your presentation. Prepare your presentation for the time allowed on the program and end on time. Note that you may have a host for your presentation that will take time to thank the local arrangements committee, other dignitaries in the audience, and may spend more time on your introduction than you planned.

One of your first assignments is to volunteer to give luncheon or dinner speeches. It is a great opportunity to meet new people, do some networking, and sell the library. When dealing with the public, many of them don't have a lot of time to listen to your message nor are they interested in the details of what you are saying, so it is essential that you have mastered Bumper Sticker Communication skills. While speaking at a luncheon, you may notice that you aren't communicating well because you are using terminology that didn't resonate with the members. Hone your pitch down to succinct and clear statements that people understand or have analogies in their own experience.

A similar event happened when, toward the end of the campaign for the Main Library Bond Issue in San Francisco, a researched and detailed case for the need for the new library was presented to the widest audiences possible. Late in the campaign there was evidence from a local pollster that the public was getting too confused about what was being said (Binder). We honed the message and it became simply, "Vote Yes for the Library."

It is often needed when one is asked questions by the general public. For example when they ask, what is a library? I often hear that a library is a facility, story hours, public programs, reading, and many other services or resources that the audience might want to hear. It is difficult to define a library without going on and on.

A succinct response would be that a library is a space (physical or virtual) to practice librarianship. This of course leads to the next question. What is librarianship? If they don't ask it directly, you can ask it and rhetorically reply that librarianship is composed of three parts. First is a mastery of the skills for the collection, preservation, organization, and dissemination of materials and channels to meet the need of the community; second is having professional ethics and values; and third is advocacy for subsidized access to information, knowledge, and learning for all. If they want to talk about librarians, lead them to the American Library Association's (ALA) professional ethics statement and other examples of the value of librarians in the community.

Sometimes you will be called upon to testify in quasi-legal proceedings. Occasionally there might be a request by a grand jury or other body who follows a rather rigid process. Often these are quite formal. Your best strategy is to try to be as prepared as possible and mostly answer their questions related to the purpose of the proceedings. On the other hand, they may be opportunities to educate elected or appointed officials so a well prepared speaker can take advantage of the situation.

If you are caught in a controversial topic that puts the library in the media spotlight, it is important that you understand that sometimes issues that you think are unimportant can be thrust front and center by the news media. These situations reinforce the need for a spokesperson who is practiced in dealing with the press, knowledgeable in the topic that caused the situation, and generally knowledgeable in the mission, vision, and goals of the library. The fact is that any deficiency in communications and knowledge in your team, staff, or supporter's knowledge on the issues will be exploited by the media since they thrive on controversy. The easiest way for the media to get a controversial story is to find an issue where two or more people disagree. Sometimes there will be a convergence of the motives of the press and the politicians who creates what I call the unholy alliance. The politicians need the press coverage to get the attention of the public and to appear to be fixing things and the press needs the politicians to fill the gap between the coverage among sports figures, entertainment figures, and murder and mayhem. This is an impetus to do your homework early. When a tidal wave of controversial media hits a library, it tends to totally distract from the task at hand and wear everyone out. It always helps to have your own stories ready to relate that can mitigate the negative views.

Stories about Yourself, Your Organization, and Your Goals

Common practice and actual research demonstrates the value of stories in human communications. They range from anecdotes to novels. Your staff should develop and practice stories about themselves. Statements about who they are, where they came from, where they are going, and what makes them special, are important parts of their story. A thoughtful and polished story that you can use for educating and networking with people is part of your homework. You, yourself having a good story can serve as a good introduction, conversation starter, and way to gain confidence in the listener.

A good story about the library is also important. This story should include the mission and vision statements, and some of the most important goals. Unfortunately, too many of them are way too long and too abstract for the average person to remember. The best rule of thumb is that you or any of your supporters should be able to recite them on the spot from memory. If that is not possible then they are too long and should be revised. It is difficult to get them simple when they go through the staff, the boards, advisory groups, and the public consideration to get everyone to agree on something simple. The tendency is to add words to make everybody happy.

This process somewhat resembles getting a bill through congress. In order to get a bill passed, everyone must be pleased, and with congress, this is sometimes done by giving a financial concession to those you want to support you. If you don't have financial incentive to get supporters, you will need to try to please everyone creating a long document. Often this requires you to use your best possible communication skills.

Understanding Financial Management Realities

It is critical for the people and organizations you are cultivating as potential donors to be confident that the library is a good steward of monies received. The government budget must be managed well with no deficits or hint of mismanagement. A foundation must be viewed as creditable in handling and reporting to the donors on the proper expenditure for the purpose for which the donation was made. Your local community foundation may agree to not only accept and manage the contributions, but they may also be a lead donor to your cause.

The library, or its surrogate, must have clear authority for the acceptance and expenditure of the funds or people will be hesitant to donate. It is also the case that donors are usually unwilling to donate to the general operation of the library, so your cause must always be for a new project so that people, corporations, and nonprofit organizations will be willing to donate funds for these projects. You also need to be aware that long-term financial planning is critical for a major project such as a building.

At the time the development program is being planned, it is critical to have an accurate, up-to-date, and well-managed financial reporting system in place. The library and its support groups must be able to retain or control the money raised for library purposes. You may be able to get grants, foundation donations, and money from book sales, but be sure that you have the authority or political influence to decide how to spend the money.

Another caution is that while you are raising more and more money from outside the normal city sources, you must keep your funding source from lowering your appropriation from public funds at the same time. One of the tactics is to have a not-for-profit support group such as the FOL or a library foundation do the money raising and handle the money. You still have to ensure that the group will spend the money on activities that support the goals of the library. You also have to ensure that the library or city has the ability to accept items or services purchased by these groups. For example many cities have a strict policy on acceptance of furniture and equipment, and other items such as books.

Determine Your Authority

Authority can be derived from a number of sources. It may be local, regional, statewide, or in some cases national. In management literature there is a lot of discussion about various types of authority but the one relevant to what we are doing is the legal authority of your position. It is very important for you to understand what your authority is at the start. Check out your job description early and if it is unclear check with the people who have the authority over you. You may need to extend your responsibilities in order to get the job done or influence the people who have the authority. It is critical that you not undertake responsibility for which you have no authority. That issue should be clarified in the agreement surrounding your appointment to the position.

ANALYZING YOUR COMMUNITY

In order to reach your intended audience, you need to identify each group and then decide the best way to reach them. These will include your elected officials, your community, and your potential donors. You will be communicating with all of these frequently, and you must consider the best way to do this. You must practice and polish your communication skills whether they are letters or formal presentations. You should get comfortable communicating with your elected officials. It is important to get your messages to people who can and will take action on behalf of the library. How to maximize your stakeholder's time, energy, and money will be discussed in Chapter 6.

Elected Officials

Figure out the motivations for the politicians and appointed officials. It is always wise to have regular communications with elected officials. While Marilyn Gell Mason was director of the Cleveland Public Library, she regularly sent personal letters to her elected officials soliciting their input as well as presenting timely information. She feels that they appreciated the personal touch. In this way, a letter about a project for which you are seeking funding will not be the first written communication they have had with you during the last six months. These letters are carefully crafted to make them interesting, cover the information with as few words as possible, and ask for their opinions when an opinion is needed.

The successful leader in public sector organizations must understand that politics is important and can use the process effectively to build a better library. They must also have a good understanding of what activities and strategies can contribute to the program to increase the level of political support in both the short term and the long term.

It is important that people involved in political advocacy tactics need to have cultural knowledge, particularly in countries that have differing systems. It is even true in different communities in the United States. Sometimes the lack of understanding gets a new person in trouble. A working knowledge of how the decision makers make their decisions is needed and also what the processes are to get something approved.

Hang out with the politicians. Go to their events and celebrations. Sit in on their meetings and observe what happens. Get to know them when they are new in office. They often don't have their agenda full and prioritized by special interests like those who have been in office for a while. You have a better opportunity to educate them at the start of their experience in politics. Being active in attending political and governmental meetings and cultural events provides opportunities for creating new relationships and strengthening existing ones. You meet people and often during times when you aren't actually involved in what is going on, you can talk with stakeholders at high levels. You need to have your sales pitch ready and tailored to interest the other person.

Users

Users of library services are the easiest to identify if they have registered for a library card and/or enter a library facility where they can see posters that communicate events and service opportunities to them. If they are registered you can use their name and address to send them mail or e-mail. If you plan to do that there should be a statement on the registration form where they can opt out of the notification system if they so desire. If you have their e-mail and permission to send them notices and service opportunities, it is easy to get in touch with them. Two-way communication with them online makes a lot of sense. The new tools for creating online communities such as blogs, listserves, discussion list, chats, and the new virtual community-building tools can play an important part in the communication with stakeholders. Several libraries have appointed an emergent technology manager to scan the tools available for services and communications and to recommend the acquisitions of ones that can be used to improve services as well as efficiency. The Public Library of Charlotte and Mecklenburg County has been a leader in technology implementation for quite some time. It is no coincidence that they are also one of the recipients of one of the 2006 National Awards for Museum and Library Service from the Institute of Museum and Library Services (IMLS). Excellent sources are found in the professional literature as well as online. *American Libraries*, *Library Journal*, *Library HiTech*, divisions of ALA, and state library associations all provide excellent opportunities for keeping up with the new technology.

Always set up a formal system for feedback from people using the library. A form headed "Compliments and Complaints" should be available and staff should be trained to encourage the public to fill out these forms. If they fill out the form and let us know how to contact them, a follow-up to them can be provided. Sometimes there would be a bulletin board where people could write their comments and staff would post a response where everyone else could see the information as well. People who prefer anonymity were given less weight since there was no way to verify their information or to provide feedback to them. While complaints often outweighed compliments, it is important to have a channel for the positive as well. The staff tends to like the system since it allows the user the opportunity to vent to someone besides the staff right there.

Community Organizations

Every community has a host of organizations and many of them would make good allies with the library for development. Sometimes it is difficult to choose the ones that have the most potential for success sharing. There are two criteria that can be applied in the process of selecting community partners. Look for organizations that have resources to share and have a willingness to share resources that you don't have such as skills in fundraising. They may have connections in the community that you don't have and you may have some connections that they don't have.

At Pike's Peak Library District (PPLD), our development of one of the very first online Community Information Systems not only gave the library something to talk about in promoting their community value but gave the library a resource that the other community agencies needed to be more successful than they were at the time. A tremendously active community-wide network was created with the library at the core of the network in an essential role in making the network an outstanding example of community networking for information and reference purposes. This network also allowed the library to make the database which was maintained by the agencies themselves through dial-up connections and then leased lines available to every person who had a dial-up access capability to the library's computer. A large critical mass was created in the application of the technology, which demonstrated the library's leadership in access to information and knowledge for the community. This system brought in federally funded positions from the Comprehensive Employment and Training Act, provided opportunities to market the library to the clients of the participants in the network, and got the library as well as the coalition tremendous publicity.

This example leads to the second criterion for successful partnerships and that is to look for organizations that have convergent goals. Sometimes it may simply be the need for publicity as demonstrated in the SFPL's participation in the National Poetry Week celebration in San Francisco. Sometimes two agencies need each other to make the case for support for educational institutions. A recent example is the creation of the Library for the City of San Jose and the San Jose State University in California.

Both libraries made the case that they needed a new state-of-the-art and larger library but neither could fund their building programs individually. By partnering over many objections of faculty and staff, a magnificent new library was built at the intersection of the campus and the downtown. It has proven to be very successful to this point. The partnership also made it unique among large city public libraries and large state university libraries. It was a huge effort and the people who provided the leadership are to be commended.

One small procedure that can communicate to potential stakeholders is reaching a *quid pro quo* on marketing with other agencies and organizations in the community. For example, many of them want to put posters on the library's bulletin board or other communications vehicles, and that is a good way to get the agency as a stakeholder. The relationship should be reciprocal, however, and if you display their materials, they should display those of the library. When your community is well informed about your plans for the project, it is time to consider how to work with potential donors. This takes time for planning.

Making Cities Stronger

Public libraries build a community's capacity for economic activity and resiliency, according to a recent study from the Urban Institute. This report adds to the body of research pointing to a shift in the role of public libraries—from a passive, recreational reading, and research institution to an active economic development agent, addressing such pressing urban issues as literacy, workforce training, small business vitality, and community quality of life.... (Urban Library Institute).

Natural Stakeholders

Get in touch with natural allies such as literacy programs, bookstores, other libraries, and community organizations such as parent–teacher groups, Kiwanis, among others. Learn the interests of different groups and target activities to meet their specific interests. In a small-town setting with a small library it is easy to communicate directly with the stakeholders. In some ways perhaps, the best libraries are in small towns where the staff know the collections, the residents, the decision makers, and can provide very personalized service. On the other hand, in the past, they were limited in the size of their collections and often in the training of the staff. These have disappeared as a liability with the growth of regional and state library networks which caused these small libraries to become less insular. The regional focus on resources allowed the sharing of strengths in each library's collection and increased the number of items available. The creation of the mega networks such as OCLC expanded the reach for title location globally. Now, with the Internet in combination with all of the above, the small library has the ability to excel in the breadth and depth of their services. They often have a higher staff to public ratio than the larger libraries and it is easier to organize smaller collections than mega collections in many facilities. However, as the community and thus the library increases in size and complexity it becomes more difficult to communicate with the stakeholders. The ability to assign individuals to stakeholder groupings becomes necessary so that you can target specific groups through differing media. For example, there is the user who is in the library regularly, ones who use it less, ones who rarely use it, and the nonuser who believes it is important to other members of their family or the community as a whole, and so on. The reason for this analysis is to develop targeted communications to each group and to create a community of each type of stakeholder. This exercise can become quite varied if the stakeholders are grouped by education, income levels, cultural groups, and on and on. At some point it becomes less productive and priority should be given to those who have strong stakeholder support. As a part of the communication process, it is important to have regular celebrations and events to get the groups together.

While they may not recognize it the library employees are also natural stakeholders. They have a vested interest in the future development of the library, perhaps more than any other group.

Organizations That Want to Ride Your Publicity Coat Tails

Another opportunity at the SFPL was the one of becoming the target of the "poetry ladies." A successful publicity campaign was underway surrounding the new main library project when a call came from some people who were promoting a national poetry day and they wanted to start with San Francisco with the SFPL as the lead local organization. This seemed to be interesting, but it didn't seem to be a priority in what was happening at that time. The ladies we called "The Poetry Ladies" were persistent and eventually won over the secretary (a tactic that will be covered under access to decision makers in Chapter 7) and a meeting was scheduled with them. They immediately demonstrated their enthusiasm and energy and they had persuaded some of the major department stores around Union Square to put their poster on their billboards for a week. Having the SFPL's name on those posters seemed a good idea, so we became a sponsor.

The outcome was that the "Poetry Ladies" convinced the San Francisco giants that we should have poetry day at the baseball stadium; and they got Alan Ginsburg, an icon from the San Francisco Beat Generation, to recite one of his poems in the stadium just before the game started. And, it was a new experience to introduce him to some 40,000 to 50,000 people since it became clear that a baseball stadium is one of world's largest echo chambers and the speaker's voice came booming back to them over the public address system. Ginsburg got wound up reciting "Howl" one of his most famous poems about the war in Vietnam, totally ignored the audience who started to yell "play ball." Ginsburg was impervious to all that was going on, a surreal event for everyone except Ginsburg. But, the SFPL not only made the local and regional news that night, ESPN said that the city of San Francisco was a very literary town.

Donors

Locating and nurturing donors is an area where it is important for you to be knowledgeable, poised, and passionate. A campaign that has professional staff will locate and research the donors for their ability to donate and will set the stage to provide the opportunity for the library leadership to give the sales pitch on the campaign. If the library or support organization does not have the ability to fund professional staff, they should look for volunteers or organizations that would do pro bono work. The staff must be very professional in their approach and thorough in identifying major donors, researching their capacity to give, their philanthropic interests, and getting them to attend a sales pitch. You may be presented with the opportunity and challenge of making the case for the campaign in about fifteen minutes. No one from CEOs and owners of major corporations to the president of your local bank has much time, so the message has to be succinct, attuned to their own goals for their businesses or families, and convey a sense that you know what you are doing. If the presentation is for a small group of financial business leaders, you should emphasize the opportunity for the library to support education and community growth. If the group is interested in history, you should emphasize the ability of the library to preserve and organize the knowledge from the past. For a literary group the importance of books and reading also needs to be stressed. It always helps to have the invitation to the group comes from a member of the group who is highly respected.

It is also necessary for you, your staff, and those working on the campaign to find out from the stakeholders and potential donors just who they may not wish to have donating to the project. They may find someone or some organization whose donation is unacceptable and these areas need to be addressed before the fund drive begins. The involvement of some corporate donors may be opposed by other stakeholders in the library. Sometimes the unions, environmentalists, or outspoken opponents of certain politicians may surface to complicate the issues.

IDENTIFY THE BARRIERS

Financial Limitations

You will be surprised to learn how many barriers there are to successful fund development. Among these are local statutory constraints on revenues for the library. In some cases, all revenue, including fines and book replacement costs, must go to the general fund and be reallocated through the budget process. Ideally, for public relations purposes, it would be easier to explain fines and fees if the person paying them could see that the money goes for more books or to replace the ones that are not returned. In fact, some people say that they believed that the money collected in fines and fees pays for the library's operation. These fees typically don't even pay the cost of collection and accounting for the money collected.

You will also find a lot of gotchas such as blanket tax reduction acts, limitations on revenue or limitations on revenue growth such as Proposition 13 in California, the Tabor Act in Colorado, voter initiatives in Oregon, and other states. These can place huge roadblocks in the path to development. These are meat ax approaches to solving tax and spending problems. Recently a local Arizona paper had a guest editorial by the chairman and executive director of the Arizona Federation of Taxpayers, a state chapter of Americans for Prosperity, titled, "Four steps you can take to bring property taxes under control." They advocate opposition to any tax increases at any level for any purpose. They portray taxes as almost evil. They don't seem to worry about where funding for public construction, services, law enforcement, judges, or any other infrastructure or operational costs will come from (Kirkpatrick and Jenney, 2007).

Watch for legal limitations on spending for lobbying and influencing public opinion. It is easy to violate the US (IRS) code concerning nonprofit organizations. If all of the revenue is to be spent on lobbying and influencing the political process then a separate (taxable) organization may need to be set up under IRS Section 503 C. The ALA just went through the process of setting up a "Professional Association" in order to avoid tax liability on their status as an educational organization. This limitation can affect any level of lobbying or campaigning from the local to the national. Seek legal advice concerning barriers to ensure you don't hit a gotcha.

It has happened that elected officials often cut the budget of a library feeling that the FOL, community donors, or other fundraising efforts will provide the needed funds. If this is the case, it is critical that the library have nonprofit organizations such as the FOL or a library foundation. They have the ability to put on events to raise money for the library, to retain the profits from such events, and to purchase goods or services that meet the library's priorities. The development and alliances with these organizations can be very delicate since at times the organization's priorities differ from those of the library director or officials. It requires clear and constant communications at the top levels of the nongovernmental organizations (NGO) and the library leadership for success. Since San Francisco is a "Charter City" under California law (the only one in California) it has greater latitude to deal with finances than any other city or county in California. This was crucial knowledge that led to the success of the recent development of the SFPL. A dedicated, determined group of networked stakeholders were able to take funding issues directly to the voters of San Francisco. Once approved by the voters they virtually guaranteed an exceptionally high level of funding for the library for fifteen years. The proposition passed in 1994 will sunset in 2010 and hence require a new action on the part of the voters to ensure the continuation of the direct funding levels of the library. In 2007, the voters approved the continuation of the revenue set aside by a large margin.

Many gotchas will exist in many communities. The fact that they exist does not necessarily prohibit the library from succeeding. In many cases they can be overcome but they should be researched early to assess the impact on the funding development program and overcoming them will have to be factored into the strategic planning. It can take years to change state statutes that provide a cap on local library revenue and a statewide referendum is so costly that other approaches must be taken. It is at this time that the library must find its real political allies.

Knowing Who to Talk to When

People or organizations exist who don't agree with your goals for the library and they often don't appear until the process is under way. A really tricky skill is the ability to determine which person or group should be central at first in your process of creating a strategic plan. Obviously, you want to have a vision that involves and is supported by the largest number of stakeholders possible. But, which group do you start with. Who should you listen to first? Are there groups that don't contribute in a productive fashion to the process? How many resources should you expend to get people involved? How about the people that have little background or knowledge in the particular topic being considered?

Most libraries have critics of their operations or goals and they often are quite visible and vocal. Sometimes they can contribute to the library, but sometimes they are more of a resource drain. Even seasoned directors can err on determining who is the most important stakeholder or group.

UNDERSTAND THE IMPACT OF CHANGE

One of the biggest drivers forcing the library to need money is the fact that rapid change in society (not the slow pace of the past) is now the norm. This pace of change requires money for new technology and new technology requires money for specialized staffing, maintenance, supplies, and training in order to meet new consumer demands such as access to the Internet in libraries. As shown by recent surveys, the majority of library users feel that libraries don't have enough user points to facilitate this access. Fortunately many of the changes are really cost-effective once the transition is made, but it takes money to make the changes.

Some of these changes have been happening for years but are still ongoing. Some are graphic to neographic content, singular processes to mass processes, mono access to multidimensional access points, single to many simultaneous users, singular to collaborative organizations, ownership orientation to access orientation, rights of ownership to licensing and stricter copyright, government mandates, self-service, experiential library, scarcity vs. overabundance, collection to access, gatekeeper to facilitator, and fortress to pipeline. It is important to include these specific change agents in your message to show the magnitude of the transition that the library must take to remain relevant. These will be expanded below.

Graphic to Neographic Content

Most libraries were created when print was practically the only media in use in the collections. It is not necessary to go through a list of the changes. We only need to point out that at one time the papyrus scroll was the only format, then the printing press came along, and then the whole electronic networked stuff appeared. My long time search for how to characterize the difference between the print world and the nonprint world came up with the concept of graphic for the print-based media and neographic for all of the others. Even though we store the representations in digital form, we still use traditional print characters for reading. So, the new media is not totally new, only parts of it. This concept evolved while thinking about one of the tours through the Louvre. In one hall the statues on one side are Greek. On the other side they are Roman. In the middle is this one solitary statue. Questioning our guide, a docent who was a friend of a friend, she shrugged and said that they couldn't tell whether it was Greek or Roman. "Besides, the Romans mostly copied the Greeks." This seemed apt. While we have new media, they still tend to mimic many of the attributes of the old. Witness the e-book. But, we can't rely on the procedures developed for the book library to manage the new media.

Singular Processes to Mass Processes

Thirty or forty years ago most libraries were like cottage industries. The books were selected one at a time by the librarians, cataloged one at a time by the librarians, and handled one at a time by the staff. As salaries for librarians and other library staff increased, this mode made the cost of operation rise exponentially. As library staff reached parity with teachers and other public service workers, the proportion of the budget required for personnel costs grew until in many libraries the norm is for the personnel budget to be over 85 percent of the budget. The only real way to decrease that percent is by automation or self service. While many libraries have been successful in implementing both strategies, many of the large libraries lag way behind the smaller ones.

Mono Access to Multidimensional Access Points

In the days of the card catalog, the average number of entries per item was usually a handful. You would have a title card, an author card (one for each author), and perhaps some subject entries if it is nonfiction. You would probably have around four cards per item as an average. As cataloging evolved and the creation of the MARC record standards by the Library of Congress more access points such as media or format were added to the bibliographic record. The basic purpose of cataloging is to provide enough information so that you could surmise that the item described is the one that you want. Depending on the size of physical collections there was some variation in the comprehensiveness of the bibliographic record.

Some studies showed that the Dewey Decimal Classification System was most effective up to 1 million items in the collection. At that point it was more effective to use the Library of Congress Classification System since it was designed to provide access to one of the largest collections in the world and is specific to the physical item. Dewey only goes to the title and some other means must be found to identify the specific copy.

In today's world with Google and digitized books freely available, you can search for any word in the item. In other words, the number of access points equals the number of words in the item. If the book has 50,000 words there are at least 50,000 access points.

Single to Many Simultaneous Users

The implementation of online catalogs expanded the number of users who could access the same bibliographic information. With the Internet it is difficult now to come up with the number of simultaneous users. Your catalog is available anywhere a person has an Internet connection or local networked workstation. It numbers into the hundreds of millions today. While some physical limitations are placed on the internal capability in the computer and network, for all practical purposes the threshold for gridlock is so high as to be practically not reachable.

Singular to Collaborative Organizations

The days of cottage industry in libraries are pretty much over except for very distinct and special collections and services. Cataloging is networked, much of acquisitions are purchased with automatic ordering, and even reference is more and more becoming a networked system. The networking that we know today in libraries really started in the 1960s when state and federal programs provided funding for starting regional library systems and other collaborative organizations. OCLC has become a huge global network based on the principle of collaboration and sharing resources to streamline and expand processes and services.

This collaboration has led to new models for service and management of library functions. New skills are needed such as contract negotiation and quality control through contractual obligations. These are very much in demand now.

Ownership Orientation to Access Orientation

A totally new method of ensuring access to journals over the last ten years is through the licensing of databases or access to indexes and other tools. The fastest growing segment of acquisitions now is the online journals and other publications. Online access to information through the library's physical network or licensing fee is pretty much standard now. The current procedure has changed many of the procedures of the library and probably saves money over time. What is lost of course is the freedom of first-use rights in the copyright act and control over the content and availability of the publications.

Rights of Ownership to Licensing and Stricter Copyright

A major shift that many librarians don't seem to notice is the fact that copyright of published materials has been changed dramatically in the last twenty years. The original concept of striking a balance between the rights of the creator and the rights of the consumer has become skewed to the rights of the creator. The large conglomerate corporations such as Disney and Time/Warner have been successful in extending both the time and content of published items. In fact, just by writing a book, an implied copyright is in place. The doctrine of first use, which generally allows one to resell, loan, and reproduce in a limited amount, has been modified in terms of other media. The librarian of today needs to be aware of these issues. Fortunately, the ALA's Office of Information Technology Policy (OITP) tracks these developments and provides information and training for librarians and their attorneys. It is in constant change, and is a constant battle by the ALA and others to protect the "fair use and first use" legal rights that have existed for centuries.

Government Mandates

While most libraries have avoided the strict oversight of the federal government that has occurred in education, they are now subject to a number of strings if they want federal money. If the money is for technology access to content, they must accept the mandate to filter the results. They may have the same requirement from their own community funders. If this is the case then someone on the staff must be knowledgeable about the issue. When a library is built or renovated, it will have to comply with the requirements of the Americans with Disability Act (ADA). During the construction of the new main library (NML) the provisions of the law was recently passed and the Justice Department, state and local governments were creating the regulations for the implementation for the mandate. The evolution of this law created a great deal of stress and expense for the NML project. For example, one of the custom build cases to house catalog cards in the special collections department had to be returned to the vendor to be resized for its area. Almost 40 percent of the open stacks were lost because of the increase in the isle widths and the shortened linear stack lengths. While the value of the bill is obvious for its ability to enhance the ability of the disabled to navigate throughout buildings, its implementation cost at SFPL was high due to the fact that it was being formulated and implemented in the middle of the NML project. It would have been very helpful to have someone knowledgeable in the act during the design stage. Other mandates from government agencies such as the Fair Labor Standards Act and Right to Work Act have changed the director's and administrative librarian's jobs immensely. It is definitely the case that what you don't know can cost you.

Self-Service

The majority of the organizations in the commercial world have gone to self-service models some time ago. Usually if you want someone else to do these tasks, you have to pay extra to implement the technology and training. Sometimes it is in money and sometimes it is simply in inconvenience. Many libraries have implemented this model very successfully.

Experiential Library

The Cerritos Public Library has billed itself as the first experiential library. Old-fashioned book libraries provide a certain experience to the users as demonstrated in the image of people quietly pursuing reading or information acquisition activities. Although probably overstated, this was certainly part of the ambiance. Even the Cerritos Public Library has a traditional reading room with dark paneled wood furniture with a fireplace with a fire to give readers a place that is familiar to them. Since the fireplace was designed and built by the Disney people, it isn't real although it looks real. People stand in front of it like it is warming them. However, the popular library of today must expand the types of experiences for the user. At the other end of the spectrum the Cerritos Public Library children's center is one of the liveliest and most interesting ones that could be imagined.

This library is the result of a complete reevaluation of library services incorporating the potential of the Internet as a service provider as well as the staff. It was inspired by a book on the experience economy which focuses on making the library user friendly and customer service oriented. The design was inspired by the Guggenheim Museum in Bilbao, Spain, and is very striking with its titanium skin glowing different colors throughout the day. The staff roams the spaces to assist patrons but can be reached via their personal communications device if needed. The children's library includes a 15,000-gallon saltwater aquarium that includes sharks and coral. It also has a fossil replica of Tyrannosaurus Rex, simulated atmospheric changes in a rain forest, and a design on the ceiling that shows the constellations in the universe. It is a very lively place and the children flock to visit that library.

Each space and function was scripted by staff and consultants. In a personal conversation the director's focus was on user-centric services which he states:

1. Links a library's effectiveness to how patrons rate their visit
2. Brings backroom staff onto the floor to maximize the personal touch
3. Promotes a multisensory learning environment, and
4. Never marginalizes the preeminence of books in the library mission.

The design was storyboarded by Disney experts and handed off to the architect to create. They created a new generation for the Internet that allows individual users to customize the display and provided individualized services. Today it is one of the most talked about libraries in the world and the number of visitors each day is astounding for a city with only 100,000 residents.

Gatekeeper to Facilitator

The library used to be your last hope. If you didn't find it at your library, you probably couldn't get it when you needed it. Inter-library loan was often slow to locate the item and even slower to borrow it from another library. When OCLC began providing access to other library's catalogs, it became much easier for you to request to borrow a copy from a known source. Then OCLC added the request function and you could ask to borrow it online. This certainly speeded up the process. Of course, now not only is the location of the item determined online, more and more of the items reside online. This allows one to get the information without any intermediary. Librarians can no longer view their role as gatekeepers. Their role is more to facilitate the user's access to information and knowledge through technology, training, and portals.

Fortress to Pipeline

Another analogy for the changes in libraries is moving from the building-based fortress image to that of a pipeline. In fact, this is pretty close to what is happening. In the fortress days you had to come there to use its facilities, you had to get permission to enter it, you paid for it through your taxes, and it was a stable, long-term operation. The pipeline existed before the Internet, but it has reached gigantic proportions since the evolution of the Internet. Trying to get relevant information or knowledge now is like trying to drink from a fire hose or big pipe. So much content is coming out that it is difficult to even assess it, let alone apply all that comes out of the pipe.

Frey's Thesis

Frey talks about some of the same issues and believes that some of them are good signs for jobs for librarians. He is convinced that the demand for global information is growing exponentially and this is setting the stage for a new era of global systems. He lists some very specific actions for librarians.

1. Evaluate the library experience
2. Embrace new information technologies
3. Preserve the memories of your own communities
4. Experiment with creative spaces so the future role of the library can define itself

His advice is very practical and includes specific actions to accomplish the goals he lists (Frey).

The Internet World

The library of today must constantly be on top of the changes in the community, the changes in the attitude of the residents, and the changes in technology. It must constantly retool its technology and its techniques. It resembles a concept borrowed from biology and other sciences, particularly DNA studies, which talks about the recombinant process.

Thomas Horan, associate professor of architecture at Claremont Graduate School, includes libraries in his thinking on recombinant institutions. He states that a recombinant library will include meaningful places, fluid locations, digital thresholds, and democratic designs (Horan). By meaningful places he means that the library has the need to understand and maintain the value of physical places as well as extend into the virtual places.

This author's description is the Library as Place (Dowlin, 2004). While this is still very important, it is also important to understand the concept of fluid locations. Libraries need to recognize that the electronic phenomenon changes the spatial glue between activities and their spatial location. In the academic world this understanding is critical for success in distance education. Libraries must also consider the digital thresholds in their design elements for parallel physical/electronic design and the thresholds that connect them.

Another element that is critical for public libraries, and to some extent all libraries, is that the library must have democratic designs. The incorporation of a range of decision makers from neighborhood activists to elected officials into the recombinant design process not only ensures a better physical and virtual design, it is critical to the strategic funding process.

Another presentation of the recombinant library concept is presented by Lorcan Dempsey at OCLC (Dempsey). With all these changes and more, it is critical that the library be in a constantly evolving mode. The bottom line is that the library will need fresh and expanding amounts of money in order to adjust to the societal changes and needs regardless of the model presented.

GET YOUR VISION OUT TO THE PUBLIC

Once you have honed your skills, vision, and message, it is time to spread the message to stakeholders and to people who can become stakeholders if sold on the program. At this stage some new skills need to be applied.

Team Building

Strategic planning for fundraising requires team building. Some of the popular history of America distorts the truth. So much is said about the rugged individual in the history of this country; and many colorful examples are reported of great persons accomplishing great tasks. On the other hand, this nation and all other nations were built by groups. The west in the United States was not settled by the rugged individuals. The fur trappers, traders, and explorers provided information and in some cases, leadership to the effort, but the actual transformation of the geography was done by groups. It was the wagon trains, the cart pullers, and other teams of people who actually settled the west.

Accomplishing a strategic project requires a group, maybe many groups. Knowledge in the process of team building is very important. It is particularly important for leaders to have knowledge for team building and organization development or at least have resources to hire people who can do that.

Team building includes tasks such as building trust, developing communications, creating camaraderie, and providing a goal focus to the group. It would be an ideal situation if you could have a position for a staff person who could be a meeting facilitator and who could help create teams. Since constant change must be the nature of the library, this takes constant planning, team building, and other group activities to be successful in the strategic program. However, you will most likely need to do it all with the people you already have. Your first task may be building their trust of you and among themselves. Sometimes trust is inherent in the position, or reputation of the leader. Most often it has to be earned. Research shows that the way to do that is to develop situations where there is a small risk and to succeed at its accomplishment. People need to feel that your motives are in their best interest as well as their own. Your values and ethics should be professional and match with those of the organization. It can take a long time to develop a trusting organization.

The second main component must be a robust, accurate, and timely communication system for those involved. The new technology can increase communication immensely. Policies, procedures, and other operational documents can easily be made available to the staff and the public. Blogs and online discussions let the employees or public contribute their thinking to the development of policies and procedures. This new technology can make a big difference. Announcements, interactive group communications development, and other team building tasks can be greatly enhanced with a good communication system for the staff and the stakeholders.

Creating the Learning Organization

According to a recent article in the new LAMA Online Journal, the involvement of the staff will get them fully engaged in the project that is needed. With the help of a person knowledgeable in organizational development, it is possible to get the staff to apply their minds and skills into shaping and supporting the project. Sometimes it takes small changes to get the staff accustomed to changing and learning. Start with something simple like rearranging the display areas. You might even want to have a staff assessment of change. Have them list the changes made in the library in the last three or five years. If there hasn't been much change you should start a program of gradually expanding change. At the same time, provide the sources or tools that the staff needs to be successful with the change. They certainly need to know the goal that is being met with the change or any other reasons behind the decision to change. It is best to get their ideas and acceptance before the change is made. One of the biggest challenges for a staff is to go from one facility to a new, larger facility without any orientation or training. At the SFPL, a training budget of $60,000 was justified for the year of the move to the NML as if going from a DC 3 airplane to a 747 with no user manuals or training. This is always a tough sell at budget time.

The NML was designed with a dedicated high technology training center for staff. When not in use for staff purposes it is available first for nonprofits or other governmental agencies (priority was given to those that had the most congruent organizational goals with the library's goals); and if there was still time, it was made available for tutoring the public or providing classes on library topics. It is very effective for the education of library staff and supporters.

One of the newest concepts in staff training is called Learning 2.0. Meredith Farkas introduces one to this concept and points to the Public Library of Charlotte and Mecklenburg's Web site as an example (Farkas, February 2007).

WebJunction just unveiled a toolkit for blended learning that should be great for staff learning programs. It allows the library to set up the content for the class, learn the tools, and handle all of the background stuff needed for blended education. Having taught in various modes throughout the career, this author is a strong believer in the blended mode for education (OCLC, 2007). An interesting updating of staff training sessions for technology upgrade is called A Roadmap to Learning 2.0 (Farkas, February 2007).

A need for person–to-person communication remains. Provide opportunities for staff and members of support groups to learn or improve their public-speaking skills. Provide them with handouts and other supporting information such as PowerPoint or a video. Provide regular briefings or online communication to keep them up-to-date. When you have a cadre of presenters, the library should issue a press release to let community groups know that the library is willing to provide speakers for their events. You can spread the message through the individual's personal touch to many more groups than with just one or two spokespeople. If you have built or located a file of these civic and social organizations, a mailing would get their attention. Don't ever underestimate the personal touch.

Personnel Management

It is critical that the personal department in the library have the ability to ensure that the selection, orientation, training, and assessment of personnel are well done. Deficiencies in the staff, whether real or perceived, will make it difficult to achieve additional funding. Constant evaluation and feedback of employee performance and user satisfaction is critical early in the strategic fundraising process. It is also important that the staff understand where the money comes from and that their attitudes and behaviors toward the stakeholders and leaders are very important to successful fundraising. Often, in larger libraries, the staff can't see any connection between what they do and the amount of funding that the library receives.

Change Management

Development programs are usually caused by a desire to change although some are designed to simply hold on to what the library has. Strategic changes need to be managed over a long term. It is necessary to include planning, communication, and regular assessment of progress. We were able to develop a very comprehensive vision and long-range plan for change at Pike's Peak Library District (PPLD). A recent review of the archival documents there impressed me with the ability the library staff and community had to develop a vision, do the plan, get the resources, and then execute the changes. Some of them happened rather quickly, some of them took place over years, a steady, consistent program to locate, educate, and serve stakeholders in the community. Many outside organizations were involved and their influence was tremendous. Having the direction established and the antenna out for resources led to many opportunities. One of them that changed not only the library and community but librarianship in general was the development of the first community/library based online Information and Referral File that had comprehensive support in the community.

It was designed and the programs were written and implemented by the staff with the maintenance of the files done by the community agencies themselves. The library had the computer resources, the trained and motivated staff, and the leadership to make this program happen. It became one of the very first online information and referral files in the world to be available to the home via dial-up networking. It was very successful in meeting the goal that the library had adopted to serve as a community information center. It was also a tremendous tool for creating stakeholders who would rally to support library funding. It also provided two other lessons: one was that the way to start a new program was to ask for staff volunteers to create a new program rather than to assign it to an existing department or function and the other lesson was that having done the homework well the money will develop. It was at that time that the Comprehensive Employment Training Program (CETA) was passed and funded by the federal government. As often was the case, the timeline for implementation of the program was short. Because the local director of the program was an acquaintance because of our community network for resource sharing, it was possible to turn in an application for federally funded employees quickly. The result was that the two volunteer librarians who had just been put in charge of the information and referral program became one of the largest departments in the library with around twenty employees.

It wasn't easy for them since the new employees had to be trained and managed. The library was also required to give these temporary employees an opportunity to fill vacancies that occurred on the staff for which they were qualified. This was a win/win all around. The library got the new program implemented in a big way, the trainees could be evaluated for their performance during training, and the best ones were hired by the library when the library had vacancies.

Strategic Planning

Various methodologies exist for creating strategic plans, so we will only point out the need for a good one before the strategic development program starts. Several areas are emphasized for a good plan. The strategy of scenario-based planning makes the most sense since it focuses on desirable outcomes and is more appropriate for a plan that supports change. The concept of a long-range plan that is based on a predictable future is not very functional anymore. You can find information on the methodology at Wikipedia although it emphasizes the military aspect. A good look at scenario planning for libraries is presented by Giesecke in the proceedings at a conference entitled Transforming Libraries (Giesecke, 1998). It is good because it is based on the future that you prefer and feel that you can create rather than a future where the library's future is created by outside forces or events.

The largest failure for strategic planning and strategic plans seems to be the fact that many organizations have never been able to create their operationalization. There needs to be an implementation plan as well as a strategic plan. The implementation plan should include benchmarks and evaluation cycles. It should also identify who does what, when, and who evaluates the whole process.

Build a "Go-to-Team"

You need a small team of people who can be consulted quickly, are willing to commit time to the development, and are willing to support your vision. They need to be the inner circle for vision building for the library. You need persons with different talents and resources but they must be people that you can totally trust. If you are really lucky you will have an angel on the team who is passionate about the library and is willing to commit time and money when necessary. This person needs to understand the big picture of the library development, be involved politically enough to influence elected and appointed officials, and be willing to learn from you about the professional aspects of the library. Ideally, that angel (or if you are lucky you could have more than one) is involved from the start. Some of the people that you need on the team are:

Community Talent. As you are creating communications and network relationships with members of the community you should always be on the lookout for talent from people outside the organization. You may not necessarily be able to, nor want to, hire them but you can get them involved by putting them on community library committees. They can often provide talent that you lack on your staff. Sometimes there is resistance on the part of the staff to outsiders becoming insiders, so the management of the situation needs to be clear to everyone involved.

Loyal Staff. While loyalty to an individual isn't necessarily the prime attribute for a successful assistant, they should be loyal to the library and to the vision and goals adopted by the policy makers. It is very dysfunctional if people in high levels in the library oppose or sandbag the efforts by the leaders to develop the library. This is a very difficult issue. It takes time to assess the individual employee's commitment to the change and development process. It is often an issue of trust. There needs to be trust in the leadership and trust in the staff. It would be surprising to find 100 percent of the library staff would be all for major change in the library. Most of them can be educated or see the benefits of the changes to their own agendas and plans. The real issue is how much effort the library can make to educate and enlist every single one on the staff. The FOL at the SFPL funded scholarships for nonlibrarian staff to attend the University of California Berkeley or San Jose State University and they did so every year. Awardees were selected based on their outstanding motivation and ability for the library. With the support to get their Masters degree in Library and Information Science (MLIS), and their commitment, they became excellent resources in the staff.

Elected and Appointed Officials. It is important that as a public official you have an attorney on your team. It was usually a city or county attorney. Often they provide guidance in legal matters that will be missed if you haven't had a good working relationship with them. You will have numerous issues to work on together or the attorney will assign someone in the office to work on to solve the problem.

Sometimes it is possible to get high-level elected or appointed officials on your team and they can be a huge asset. On the other hand, they rarely have the library as their priority for time and money so their inclusion must be balanced.

An important member of your team has to be the person who can extend and manage your communications capability. If you consider that communicating with as many stakeholders as possible as one of your priorities, you must have someone to deal with it in a professional skilled way. Since there are only twenty-four hours in a day and you have a multitude of issues and people that need your attention, you need someone who has your complete trust. You must trust them to deal with situations in a way that you would handle it or perhaps even better. A number of very talented Community Relations Officers (CROs or public relations people) exist and they are not only worth the cost for the position, they are people who strengthen your ability to obtain and leverage funds. If your person is a librarian, they must develop the skills of a public relations person and if they are public relations they need to have extensive knowledge of the library.

Project Grant Creator. Almost all academic institutions and some cities or counties have specialized staff to work with departments to get grants from governmental agencies as well as private donors. Often they are in quasi-public agencies like a foundation so that they don't have the constraints of dealing with regularly budgeted agency funds. They can be a really good resource, and it is worth your while to cultivate a relationship not only with the person assigned to your library or agency, but also the director of the foundation. Sometimes their priorities are set by someone at a higher level than you, but since they must get much of their operational funding from the overhead charges on all grants, they are almost always willing to work with you.

Preparing grant proposals gets easier and easier as more of them are prepared and submitted. One of the most active programs for library strategic development is in the province of Ontario in Canada that provides a good model for similar operations in the United States (Ontario). If you don't have access to development staff at a higher level, you need to find a person that will do the work for the library. Often talented grant writers are willing to work on a contract basis that might be part-time or for a specified duration. This is a good application for outside funds such as those from the Friends of the Library. It is always a good strategy to invest discretionary funds such as those from outside agencies in activities that will generate more funds such as grants.

Media Relations

It is important that the library has the ability to cultivate relations with the news media. It is best to do this when there isn't a crisis. Most of the media are willing to provide coverage, stories, and promotional activities with libraries in their area. Have media relations on the list of responsibilities of the Community Relations Office as a regular program and track the success. If you wait for some kind of a crisis, you will find yourself on the defensive much of the time and that is never a good position for a positive media message. You must deal with the news media fairly and evenhandedly. It is easy to get into providing preferential communications to the media that seems the most helpful or supportive, but one must be careful not to make enemies among the other media outlets.

A challenge in this virtual age is to find the media dissemination footprint that is identical with your political base or funding base. As the media becomes more regional, national, and global in scale it is difficult to get local communication channels through the traditional news media and public service media. At the SFPL, one of the reasons for this author's energetic involvement in the creation of the Great Bay Area Library Council (GBALC) was to network the libraries in a grouping that had geographic boundaries that could match the San Francisco Bay area media footprint.

The realization that this was a factor in our strategic fund development became clear when the San Francisco 49ers football team had a promotion with the SFPL to entice children to read. They announced through the media that kids who were in the library summer reading program and read x number of books could get tickets to a

49ers' game. They didn't indicate that it was only for kids who used SFPL. Other bay area libraries were overwhelmed with requests for information and signup opportunities from all over the bay area and beyond. One of the goals for GBALC was to coordinate promotions that were bay-wide rather than just city by city. GBALC programs and funding are now taken over by the Regional Library Service Systems in the bay area that are comingling due to need for coordination and funding pressure by the California State Library, which is the major source of funding for the California Regional Library Systems.

UNDERSTANDING AND CULTIVATING RELATIONSHIPS

One of the most effective ways to cultivate relationships is to be active in attending political and governmental meetings and cultural events. This provides opportunities for creating new relationships and strengthening existing ones. From this group you will be looking for both donors and volunteers to help you with finding funding for the project. During these events you meet people and often, during times when you aren't actually involved in what is going on, you can talk with stakeholders at high levels. You need to have your sales pitch ready and tailored to interest the other person. An active library as something of interest for everyone and starting new ventures provides something to talk about with other people. New technologies in libraries have revolutionized services and access. These new services being added or being proposed will give you something to talk about at events making your listener aware of the growth going on in the library. Although some people seem reluctant to some changes, most people are at least curious and most will be very excited about the prospects for the future.

You need to match your conversations with what they are going to be most interested in discussing. Starting off with some knowledge of the people with whom you will be talking is a good idea, but if you don't know their hobbies or specialized interests, you can find these out in the conversation. Focusing on their interests, you can ask for their assistance in solving a problem, starting a new program, or simply adding one new recruit. Since people are healthier and living longer, there is a significant trend by people who retire and volunteer to help their favorite cause. Many people like libraries and enjoy spending time in them. If you ask these people for help and then give them something to do, you will be surprised how many people will help. When they are volunteering you also have the opportunity to educate them on the library's program and development. This will help you build relationships. Edward Evans contends that creating relationships is the key to fundraising (Evans et al., 2000, p. 471).

One cautionary note is that you will be educating people all the time on what you will be doing to improve services and particularly access to the collections and beyond. So you need to remember that most of your community really doesn't understand the library, its functions or its service. Some of the time you may be defending your position simply because they don't understand the library. Neither educating your community nor defending your position should bother you. Your project will improve the lives of people in your community and their attitudes are not directed at you personally.

Differences in Groups or Organizations

It is important to be able to work with many individuals in groups for communication purpose. The library needs to sort out what media should be used for which groups.

Politicians are often different than community leaders who are different from educators and so on. Learn the normal mechanisms that they use to get their communications.

Development Departments of Parent Organization

Often there are departments within the library's parent organization that have the responsibility for development of the city or university. Your efforts need to be coordinated with them and an alliance should be reached when possible. They have staff, training, and connections that can be very helpful. On the other hand, they can be problematic when their responsibility is interpreted as development of the whole and not the department's or program's.

Museums

Collaboration such as the Colorado Digitization Project that brought together the public libraries and local history museums with funding from the IMLS to create a statewide digitized historical collection project brought many new stakeholders into the library arena. IMLS wants successful grant management and collaboration among libraries, museums, and other cultural institutions. Museums often bring a different constituency to the library's stakeholder groups. Small community museums often have a passionate following who are dedicated to the collection and preservation of historical artifacts, yet don't have the training or tools to organize and inventory those artifacts. The library is a natural partner and with the strong support for collaboration between libraries and museums by the IMLS, there are significant funds available.

Library Schools or Other Schools with Student Resources

A significant number of schools for library science came from the leadership of library directors from public and academic libraries. In the early years there was a strong cross-fertilization of ideas between those organizations that laid the foundation for much of library science. Today, the practical experience and internship opportunities as well as special projects by Library and Information Science (LIS) students provide a pool of talent and energy to help in the development program of the library. You often have the opportunity to serve on an advisory committee for a LIS which will give you the chance to not only help guide the LIS program but to solicit student or faculty expertise and time to your development program.

Corporate Leaders and Influential Citizens

The library should have a membership in the local Chamber of Commerce. Sometimes their bylaws don't allow governmental agencies to be full members but most of the time the library can be an affiliate member. A chamber provides many opportunities to met and educate leaders from the corporate and business world. The director or other library staff members should serve on committees in which they have an interest. Through the work of the SFPL's library foundation, the person who chaired the NML private funding campaign was well connected with community leaders such as Charles Schwab of the Schwab Corporation, Doris and Don Fisher of the Gap Corporation, and others. They all made huge contributions to the libraries development program. The support of Landor and Associates to the library for a branding campaign, which changed the brand of the SFPL, is discussed in the next chapter.

Local Foundations

If your community doesn't have a foundation center that is part of the National Foundation Center you should work with a local foundation to start one in your library. It will get your local foundation involved as well as provide a service to your community and give you direct access to the directories and other information. If you have a local chapter you should join them so that you can attend their workshops and use their resource materials.

Angels

People who go way beyond the normal level of enthusiasm, support, and tenacity may be described as angels. Treat them as treasures and always be on the look out for new ones.

Muscle People

Muscle people are those who have inordinate power, respect, and authority in the political world and in the world of people who believe in philanthropy as a civic duty. Obtaining support from elected officials such as the chairman of the Board of Supervisors can help move mountain size barriers. Developing a working relationship with a member of the Board of Supervisors will help when bills are going to cause chaos. If this person understands the situation well, they may be able to get the bill pulled from consideration.

On the other hand they may be too helpful. Once, a president of a Board of Supervisors, who was very supportive of the library and always willing to listen, was asked to put the strategic plan on the agenda. It seemed reasonable that when it came up for a vote, the library director would have the opportunity to impress the people in the room with our outstanding planning ability. What happened was that the president wanted to get it passed with a minimum of fuss or opposition, so it was placed on the consent calendar which contained ceremonial items or other items for which there wasn't any interest in debate or discussion. It passed in seconds without even being visible. All that was left was to thank the supervisor, having learned another lesson in politics.

It is also important to recruit people who are not elected or appointed officials but have strong political, personal, or financial influence with their peers as well as the officials. When they become angels it creates magic.

Devils

Devils are people who make a hobby or even a career in attending all possible events of the library and commenting on practically everything on the agenda whether they know anything about it or not. It is very difficult to deal effectively with them. They may constantly release slanted information and even file frivolous lawsuits that take money and people's time from the library's purpose. If one uses the rational view of these people, you would bring them into the organization by appointing them to advisory committees or some other involvement as a stakeholder than the one they are. On the other hand, that strategy may just increase their ability to be effective in opposing the library's program. It's a difficult decision.

LEADERSHIP AND SUPPORT FOR FORMAL SUPPORT GROUPS

FOL, library foundation, and Junior FOL, literary clubs, volunteers, and neighborhood library councils are all important support organizations for the library. You should set up as many of the above groups possible and perhaps more that are specific to your community. They can all be effective in raising funds, expanding the communications program of the library, volunteering, and advocacy for the library's case statement for development. All of these activities are important but the biggest payoff is when the groups realize that they are at their most effective when what they do supports the strategic development program. Educating these folks require work on the part of library leadership and staff. They need to be involved in the vision and goals of the library or they will think up their own goals for the specific organization which may be counter-productive to those of the library or might divert resources outside of the strategic path. As the library leader you must be prepared to spend time in the process of educating the members of these groups, building the organizations goals and objectives, and keeping the groups and their members informed at all times. The closer these organization's activities are to the core of the library's vision and goals, the better chance of success for the library. Sometimes there are tensions between these organizations and the library staff. Often the staff doesn't understand the roles of these support groups, or they may have other personal or group goals, which can create a schism in the presentation of the strategic library development program to the public.

It is preferable to have a library foundation separate from the FOL group. While these need to work collaboratively, they have different missions of support. The foundation participants are more willing to provide money than their time and are more willing to provide volunteer time and small amounts of money.

Friends groups raise money and, through their activities, they are strong advocates for library development. Most of their members are more interested in small donations and volunteer services. They do not expect to provide large amounts of money from their own pockets or to solicit their personal or business friends for donations. They happily spend many hours on committees and are very much interested in the governance activities of the group.

You may need to reinvigorate the FOL, a library foundation, Junior FOL, and book or literary clubs. Some of them may not be knowledgeable in the library's mission or vision. It is important to have good communication with these groups to ensure assistance, talent, and support for the library's development. These organizations are also good sources for volunteers to give a hand to library activities. Their roles will be discussed in more detail in the next chapter.

EXTERNAL ORGANIZATION DEVELOPMENT

In systems theory there is the concept of the closed system and the open system. If you have little or no energy or new resources from external sources, you have a closed system. These systems tend to entropy and given enough time to die. Open systems are those that have few barriers between the energy flow from the outside to the inside and in the opposite direction. While it is almost impossible to have a totally closed system for very long, many libraries in the 1970s and before seemed to prefer to be insulated from the community in which they existed. In the late 1980s and in the 1990s more and more libraries realized that it was important to involve the community in their organization and the energy flow through the boundaries increased in these libraries. Obviously, you don't want a totally closed system since it will entropy, but you don't want a totally open system because someone has to be in control of the operations and resource allocation of the library.

Open systems take a lot of energy and time for maintenance of the system. If you involve everyone in the community in every decision, you will not get a lot done. Most people really don't want to tell you how to run a library, they just want it to meet their needs. There are some people who do want to tell you how to run the library and it is sometimes a challenge to separate the people with honest intentions from those who thrive on the attention that is given to critics of a public institution whether these folks know what they are talking about or not.

Create New Stakeholders

This is almost like missionary work, or at least sales. After you have assessed the different stakeholder groups for their potential for support, you should focus on the ones that can provide the starting funding. You should assess the elected and appointed officials with authority over the library. Include those around the elected officials such as their campaign managers (handlers), funders, and influencers. Often you can be a lot more effective working with their aides. When trying to become known to a new elected official, cultivate a trusting relationship with their aides or other people in the office. You will find that often the person at the front desk who controls the appointment book for the elected official can be educated in the importance for their boss to meet with you.

The concept of audience mapping in order to target your communications after you have had a generalized library support meeting is a good one. The Public Library Association (PLA) *Toolkit for Advocacy* has a variety of exercises and strategies for creating strong advocates with the different segments of your stakeholders. The creators of the *Toolkit* at the Metropolitan Group have an excellent record of helping create advocates and raising money for libraries and similar organizations (Metropolitan Group). At $90 it is a real bargain and is very clear and straightforward in the concepts and techniques that they have developed. At a recent ALA conference they presented several programs on fundraising for libraries.

Build Alliances with Stakeholders

Many businesses are willing to provide resources to a library fundraising effort. This is a long tradition in the public broadcasting world. Most of these donors prefer to provide volunteer work by their employees or products and services that they normally provide. That way they get a triple return. They get to charge it as a business expense, it positively affects the tax bite, and they get good publicity.

When you have events for the various groups of stakeholders, always provide some food and entertainment. It is usually possible to tap into local companies to provide the food and other refreshments. News media personalities will often volunteer to be the Master of Ceremonies. Cultivate a relationship that will provide a long-term commitment from the supporters of the event. Check to see if there are any grand openings of a new restaurant or coffee shop coming up around the time of your event.

One of the images in this author's vision of the new building was that it would convey the style of an Italian piazza in the center atrium and traffic area. The architects knew that there was a process used in Venice centuries ago to provide a long lasting coloring into the plaster on the walls using coffee grounds. Starbucks was opening a new coffee shop near the construction site of the new library in San Francisco. Starbucks not only provided the coffee grounds for the plaster on the walls they provided free coffee for staff meetings and training events at the library. They were also willing to provide the coffee service for public events. They claimed later that that new store was the fastest growing one in their chain. A new building provides many opportunities for such support for the library. In a way it is the opportunity to renew the library's vision and energy.

Build Alliances with Neighborhood Organizations

Actively seek out and cultivate partners in neighborhoods and community organizations. This is where a good online Information and Referral index on the library's computer system is a great help. The library and the Urban League may allow you to develop a very beneficial relationship that will bring in new users who are from minority groups into the communication network of the library as well as into the doors of the libraries.

Take a directory of neighborhood organizations (make your own directory if there isn't one) and use it as a checklist for organizing your program to reach out as broad as possible. The organizations should be ranked according to their ability and interest to support the library development program as a starting point. It is important for you to ensure diverse, broad representation on library committees, and support groups. You should attend neighborhood planning hearings, neighborhood social events, community service fundraisers, fairs and festivals, and block parties.

FINAL KITCHEN CLEANING

It is important that the public perceives the library as well managed and organized. Be sure and assess the current sources of funding for their ability to grow, eliminate overly expensive or ineffective programs, use technology or revised procedures to increase efficiency, and provide a clear vision for the future. Showing that you have shared the costs with other libraries or networks and that you have been effective at getting outside funding is a plus.

Now that we have cleaned out the kitchen, it is time to add equipment to make us more effective and efficient.

4

Getting Good Equipment: Skillets, Pots and Pans, Knives, and Cookbooks

This chapter describes some of the tools that need to be in the kitchen in order for a fundraising chef to be successful. These tools include technology, techniques, and methodology. Most of them are ones that you will use regardless of the specific recipe that you are using. Communication channels, like the Web site, should be multipurpose like the other tools in a kitchen. Spoons, cutting boards, or skillets can be used for many different food preparation tasks, and your communication tools are equally multipurpose.

Because of their importance, communication tools are the area on which we will spend the most time and we will especially focus on the new media. We do need to consider ongoing programs for communication with the news media regardless of the media used and we need to briefly talk about tools (programs) that aren't necessarily media specific.

It is important to realize broadcast communication such as flyers, newsletters, TV or radio doesn't ensure listening or action on the part of the receiver. Effective communication is cyclical, not one way. Feedback should be built into the communication system since the only way to be sure communication has occurred is to observe a change of behavior in the recipient. The lack of accurate, timely feedback is most often the cause of communication failures. Fortunately, there are now tools that can be mastered to maximize communication with stakeholders through their ability to invite and collect feedback. Evans et al. contends that one of the most common problems in "hearing" a message is the listener's assumption that they know the subject, it is uninteresting, or it is of no concern to them (Evans et al., 2000, p. 312). When your goal is to get the receiver engaged in your issue the responsibility for effective communication is your responsibility.

While it is relatively easy for a skilled communicator to make libraries interesting and to convince people that libraries are relevant to them or their friends and family, it is much more difficult in the library business to get them to realize that they may know little or nothing about the operations or funding needs for the library. Many people feel that they are experts based on personal contacts with the library. Often, this is the biggest detriment to a development program.

We will start with a Community Relations Office (CRO), move to traditional communications technology (around for thirty years or so), formal support groups such as the Friends of the Library (FOL), a library foundation, and others. We will then consider communication tools and techniques such as branding, bumper sticker communications, marketing and advocacy, dealing with the news media including media storm firefighting and tried and true fundraising techniques that can be applied to libraries. We will finish the toolkit with the new media (less than ten years old) and scope out some uses that maximize their value to the development program.

COMMUNITY RELATIONS OFFICE (CRO)

Regardless of the message and the specific need for funds, the library must have a good program of community relations. The purpose of a Community Relations Office (CRO) is to provide a consistent, effective communications program with the community and perhaps beyond. In the corporate world it is called public relations or marketing, but the public often feels that term is too corporate in governmental circles. Many people take exception to spending public funding for marketing of tax supported services. A CRO is much easier to defend to elected officials and the public than a marketing campaign. A successful program must be consistently funded and should be managed by a person with sufficient skills, education, and experience to be effective. This person should be responsible for the management of the program, be able to operate somewhat independently, and they must be strongly connected and supportive to the strategic level of the library management and leadership.

Sometimes there is conflict with members of the staff who feel that the priority of a CRO should be getting information out about the public programming that is scheduled for the public. This is certainly understandable but it should not be at the expense of the strategic communications program. In a large active library there is an overwhelming amount of program information. It may seem impossible for the library to target their program information to the people who want or need it. If you have a lot of events at different venues, it takes a lot of posters, flyers, and other traditional media to get the word out. The tendency is to make posters or flyers about the multitude of program opportunities and hope that the people who are interested would see the media and be in the right place at the right time. This can be problematic because of the bureaucracy involved.

If the governing agency such as a city or county requires the printing or approval for content to go through an office over at city hall or someplace away from the library's management, it can slow down the process and require additional work to get the material out. In looking at library Web sites it is interesting how higher level governments sometimes intrude into the navigation of the library's Web site in order to get credit. While it may be good for the agency to ensure that the information seeker knows that they exist and have a governing relationship to the library, it can complicate the site for the person seeking information from the library.

The CRO needs to be able to manage the creation, packaging, and dispersion of information through the appropriate channels quickly. This calls for a capacity to understand the roles of the different channels and their effectiveness for accomplishing the task at hand and to manage them in a way that the communication supports the library's strategic goals. Every piece of publicity should have the brand identifier on it so that the viewer or reader understands that it is a program of the library. All publicity for programs presented by the library must convey the fact that they are library programs. That not only increases the public relations for the library, but also creates a sense that the library is an active community agency. A variety of programs also support the mission of the library by providing access to information and knowledge.

FORMAL SUPPORT GROUPS

Librarians need to enlist the aid of support groups outside of the jurisdiction of the library. The most recognized is the Friends of the Library (FOL).

Friends of the Library

Most libraries have a FOL, and if yours doesn't, this may be one of the first activities in your planning activities. An active Friends group provides an excellent foundation for supporting and advocating the vision of the library. You can learn about all you need to know about Friends groups at the Web sites for Friends of the Library USA (FOLUSA) and American Library Association (ALA). The Web site for FOLUSA also has good information on fundraising and advocacy. It is important that your local Friends group connect with FOLUSA in order to add your enthusiasm to the national program and to learn from the knowledge on the site. ALA and FOLUSA have entered into a contract for FOLUSA to manage the ALA Trustees Association (ALTA) which has been a much needed partnership for years. The joining of the two groups will provide more resources to accomplish the goals of each group and will avoid competition for membership as well as eliminate the confusion as to who does what.

Most states have statewide organizations as well. Some people don't realize that the funding and support for libraries involve commitments to multiple levels in order to be the most successful. While the local organization is most often the focus for the enthusiasm and support of the local community, they need to be networked with state and national library advocates as well.

The FOL is an excellent source for generating leverage money, recruiting and developing advocates, providing a good communication network with supporters, providing community perspective to library leadership, and many opportunities to build the library family through celebrations. But they do more than just support and advocate for the vision; they help build it through their participation, their fundraising, and their enthusiasm. There are thousands of members of FOL groups throughout the country and they are a joy to work with. There are auxiliary benefits that are often not recognized. The FOL members provide entry into other cultures, organizations (especially business), and networks. Their introduction of you and your library to their communities and personal friends can provide a real jump-start to your community development program. The FOL are also a potential source of people as volunteers. They can provide talent that the library can't afford to hire, or perhaps can't even locate. Your FOL can become one of the most potent political groups in your community. Many members develop long-time commitments to the group, their projects, and to the library.

It is essential to spend time with the FOL. They need to be early supporters and shapers of the vision for the library in order to ensure as rich a vision as possible and to be enthusiastic stakeholders. They are different than taxpayers or users in that they voluntarily give their time and money to support the library. An administrative staff member should have the responsibility for active coordination of information and program with the Friends to ensure that all are on the same page.

Friends are doers and like to be active in helping the library do auxiliary activities such as book sales and other fundraisers. It is fairly common for the FOL or volunteers to operate a gift and a book shop in the library to provide souvenirs for the visitors, the sale of books donated to the library that the library can't use, and raise some money for library programs. Often the profits go to advocacy programs for the libraries. If monies from the Friends are used to support political advocacy as defined as lobbying by the Internal Revenue Service (IRS), the library and the FOL should obtain professional assistance in managing the funds in order to retain the nonprofit status of the organization. The current rule of the IRS is that advocacy that they call lobbying, which is when the group or members seek to influence policy or legislation for the library, can spend up to 20 percent of its yearly expenditures or activities if their annual expenditures do not exceed $500,000. The formula changes if the amount is higher changes often with the tax code. You can get a sense of the limitations on the table on the IRS Web site (www.irs.gov).

Library Foundation

Another important support group is a library foundation. The foundation's operations appeal to a different type of person as individual members and board of directors than the FOL. It is more typical that foundation members are more willing to donate their money than their time and are more interested in supporting a specific project for a specific length of time such as a new building or furniture campaign. While the leadership can be quite stable, the participants may shift as different goals are set. Hopefully, the president of the foundation will be a person who has a track record for raising money for community cultural organizations or other community fundraising. Their success rate is increased if they have the means and willingness to contribute major dollars to the campaign. This makes them more creditable when they ask their friends or colleagues for their donations. Members of a foundation board are expected to be major contributors to the campaign as well as having the ability to convince others.

The Web site for the Wyoming State Library (WSL) is a good source of information (www.wsl.state.wy.us). The pages were put together in 2007 in support of the effort to increase foundation support for the WSL and the public libraries in the state. The statement on ethics of the individual foundation board member, which they adapted from an earlier manual for the Indiana Public Library Board, is worth a look. It states:

As a member of the Foundation, I will:

- listen carefully to the board members who are my teammates.
- respect the opinion of other board members.
- respect and support the majority decision(s) of the board.
- keep well-informed of developments that are relevant to issues that may come before the board.
- participate actively in board meetings and actions.
- call to the attention of the board any issues that I believe will have an adverse effect on the library.
- always work to learn more about the board member's job and how to do the job better.

As a member of the Foundation Board, I will not:

- be critical, in or outside of the board meeting, of fellow board members or their opinions.
- promise prior to a meeting how I will vote on any issue in the meeting.
- interfere with the duties of the library director or board or undermine their authority.

Some people enjoy participating in both organizations and this is a positive in that there is a greater ability for the two organizations to work on some projects together and it increases communication between the two groups.

Junior Friends

Some libraries have active Friends for different stakeholders such as children, and these can be effective for connecting children to the library in order to educate and entertain them. It also should create present and future advocates. The Southbury Connecticut Public Library has a great program going for Junior Friends and their Web site (http://www.biblio.org/Southbury) is very good at leading kids to safe sources.

Staff Associations

You may have employees who want to network and support the library with activities outside of their work responsibilities. If that is the case they can be a helpful communication channel and provide community connections as well.

Volunteers

An active volunteer program can increase the ability for a library to expand its services and programs beyond what is afforded by the budget. A volunteer program needs to be managed by the library; the volunteers need to be trained and oriented, and need to understand their responsibility to the library. The library must have a policy on the recruitment, use, and training of volunteers. You should have a written contract of duties and responsibilities for the volunteer and the library's training and support service to the volunteer. They need orientation and training, and must have a mentor or coordinator on staff. They need a recognition program for their efforts that will celebrate their contribution to the library. The concept of a written agreement may seem strange and you may question if people will agree to such a formal approach; however it creates a better commitment on the part of the volunteer and on the part of the library. Library staff should be informed of the job of the volunteers and the volunteer can be held accountable to the staff member who is managing the program.

It is discouraging for the volunteer if staff makes them feel unwanted and not valuable to the library's services and it is discouraging to staff if volunteers aren't willing to be trained, nor acting responsibly in showing up when they are scheduled. Many libraries show volunteer opportunities on their Web sites. This should show how volunteers are used and for what library functions. Your volunteers may also be members of the Friends group if they are interested in group activities. In fact, your Friends group may be the best group from which to recruit volunteers for the library.

Staff

It is critical for any library that undertakes a development program to have a staff development program as an important part. The employees of the library are in daily communications with the different stakeholders and they need not only to have the training, motivation, and resources to complete their jobs, but also need to know the overall picture. They need to be brought into the planning process early so that they can contribute with their ideas and thinking. Attention needs to be made to team building and service goals. A number of training and communication devices such as regular memos, e-mails, and weekly management meetings are available to regular meetings of the entire staff including to all day training days. Obviously, it becomes more difficult the larger and more dispersed the staff is. Then you may need to have a polished presentation to emphasize the status of the strategic development plan for the times when the entire staff is together. You should definitely use the new tools to increase the communication ability. Online classes for the staff, regular updates via e-mail and Web site postings, podcasts, Wikis, and all those new techniques should be explored and assessed for effectiveness. As more and more of the options are used, it becomes more and more critical to stay on message concerning development of strategic plans for funding. It is easy to have too much communication, cross communication, and downright inaccurate communication today.

An old fashioned way to educate or train library staff is the use of learning circles. During the time of the introduction of library automation at the Pike's Peak Library District (PPLD) it was obvious that the ability to use the El Paso County's mainframe computer through leased lines also brought tools that the staff could use for more efficient communication. The use of e-mail, word processing, and elementary network search tools could increase the writing and communication ability of all library employees. The issue was how to get them trained in their use and oriented to the benefits of the program. Being creative, we came up with the concept of learning circles.

The implementation was quite simple; it started with the director's wife getting trained in the tools by Digital Equipment Company, which was the manufacturer of the computer. Three staff members volunteered to take classes from her and then to each teach three more people. They were given time from their normal duties to learn. In that way many of the employees became adept in the use of the tools and over time the online skills spread to all the library staff. There is a more current example at the Web site for the Tufts University program called the Massachusetts Campus Compact (Tufts Massachusetts Campus Compact).

Recognition programs for outstanding supporters. Regular awards for outstanding members of the FOL, the foundation, staff members, and volunteers should be part of the CRO program. Have a reception or some kind of public program and give an award. You can often find sponsors who will pay for the food and other costs of the event. The Alliance Library Association presents a Trustee of the Year Award that is sponsored by Nu Way Transportation, Inc. Their Technology Award is sponsored by Pearl Technology. In addition, they provide a number of other awards to members and supporters of the system (Alliance Illinois Advocacy Day).

COMMUNICATION TOOLS AND TECHNIQUES

Kristin Yiotis states that there are differences between public relations, marketing, and advocacy. In her words, public relations concerns long-term relationship building—the ongoing interactions with people beyond the library community. Marketing relates to a specific transaction; you market a specific program to a target population to bring about a specific transaction. An example would be marketing the summer reading program to school-aged children or their parents to encourage reading. Advocacy involves advancing a cause or proposal through persuasive argument. The cause or purpose must have a clear focus—a problem defined in terms of the community served, such as what the library can't do because it doesn't have the resources. The cause must have a solution—such as if the bond measure passes then the library can better serve the community. The cause must include a call to action—therefore, please vote yes on the library bond measure, or vote yes on the library funding bill. Kristin goes on to talk about the steps to accomplish advocacy very clearly (Yiotis, 2007).

It isn't necessary to differentiate among these three terms for the purposes of this book since there is so much overlap in the tools and techniques. However, since there are elements that are different in terminology, methodology, and advocates they must be coordinated to support the strategic development program. The goal is to keep it simple in this book. It is helpful to consider some of the different facets of a good communication program. Like a good diamond, there are many facets to look at. These range from a major branding campaign to Bumper Stickers.

An example of Bumper Sticker communication is sometimes needed when you are asked questions by the public. For example when they ask, what is a library? Much of the time the library is described by its attributes such as a facility, story hours, public programs, reading, and many other services or resources it provides. It is difficult to be comprehensive without going on and on. A succinct response would be that a library is a space (physical or virtual) to practice librarianship. This of course leads to the next question. What is librarianship? Librarianship is composed of three parts. First is a mastery of the skills for the collection, preservation, organization, and dissemination of materials and channels to meet the information, knowledge, and reading needs of the community; second is having librarians that have professional ethics and values; and third is advocacy for subsidized access to information, knowledge, and learning for all in the community.

Most librarians don't think of the library's need for an identity like a company or business. Even though a library is not in competition in a normal business sense centered on buying and selling services or goods, a library is in competition with a host of organizations and activities for a person's time. Time is the most valued asset for many people in today's society. One of the reasons that the traditional library lost market share in the 1970s and 1980s was because the traditional "you had to go to the library to use its services" took time for people to locate the library, come to the library, and take the time getting the information or other resources that they were seeking. While there were people who had the time or were willing to give it a priority over other activities, the fact is that with the entertainment media and all of the other activities in competition, the number of users of libraries per capita was dwindling. Numerous articles in the library literature decried the loss of usage to book stores, TV games, and so on. Statistics that truly reflect the library usage in all its forms, including electronic, show a dramatic upswing in library usage with the addition of electronic transactions. Now the Internet makes library services ubiquitous throughout the country. The Internet-focused library saves people a great deal of time and money.

Part of the communication process is to understand and influence the perceptions of the stakeholders. Even though the book is increasingly becoming a smaller percent of library activities, there are still people who feel that it should be the only function of the library. Those people may be quite dogmatic and they reinforce the view that the library is less relevant to their information and knowledge needs in the Internet age. While it is the case that many people view the library as an institution with responsibilities in the community that extend beyond the traditional ones, many people think of the books first. While they are still important, their share of the service statistics continues to decline.

Branding

In the contest for people's attention and support, the people's perception of the library becomes important. This is where the brand comes in. What is the image in the brand, in marketing terms of the library? Is it the book which many libraries employ in their logo, or a building which may be a familiar site in the community, or perhaps a combination of elements? It is important that this brand (using a commercial sense) is strong, identifiable with that particular library, and prominent in the communication program. The funding sources and needs must be linked to that library in the minds of the public. The brand equals the image and the image equals the brand. While the look of a soft drink "brand" may be a can of soda pop or the company logo, the image from the series of commercials where people from many lands and cultures came together and sang is the warm and fuzzy image for this company. The history of the development of the theme "It's the Real Thing" campaign is an excellent lesson. The song, "I'd Like to Buy the World a Coke" even made the popular music charts and is consistently cited in advertising surveys as one of the best commercials of all times. The whole saga of creating it is a lesson in creativity, doggedness, and teamwork (Coca Cola).

As the public relations program for the PPLD became very active in the late 1980s, it became clear that the brand needed changing. When the main library of Colorado Springs was opened in 1968 it was named the Penrose Library in honor of the man who was the founder of Colorado Springs and the creator of the El Pomar Foundation which funded the architect, the building consultant, and the construction costs for the new library. All of the signage and publicity referred to the Penrose Library rather than to the Pike's Peak Regional Library District. As the PPLD grew, adding branches, bookmobiles, and other services, people were confused about Penrose's relationship to PPLD. The residents of Colorado Springs didn't know about PPLD and people looking for the PPLD would call from a small nearby town named Penrose and say they were in Penrose but they couldn't find the library. It was critical that the brand and publicity emphasize that Penrose Library is operated and financed by the PPLD rather than the city of Colorado Springs, or Penrose.

The brand of the SFPL in 1987 was around fine printing. The library does have a collection of fine printing and rare books, but the majority of the collection and the services do not involve them. That is a very small part of what the library does. It was very difficult to get funding, either public or private, for all of the other services and resources as many of the public perceived the main library as only for special collections.

One of the most significant alliances for SFPL came about through the very creative mind of one of the public relations consultants. When she learned that we needed to change the image of the library, she realized that the library needed a "branding campaign" but the library didn't have any money to hire someone to do the design. She thought about the problem and came back with a solution. It sounded pretty far out; but it was worth the effort to try.

She had developed a contact with the administrative assistant of the CEO and principle owner of an advertising agency—at that the time the seventh largest in the United States with headquarters in San Francisco. She convinced the assistant to place a gold fish bowl filled with water and a live goldfish on the CEO's desk one morning before he came to work. In the bowl was also a miniature whiskey bottle with a small note in it. It floated in the water like a bottle in the ocean. When he arrived, he opened the bottle and read the note, which said, "Help, the library needs an identity."

Although he was semi-retired, he still controlled the company. Within hours the VP for creative design called and said that the CEO told him that he wanted to help the library and it was the his task to find out what we needed and to provide it through the company at no charge. The library became a client of the firm, where the library staffs were all treated as big bucks clients. It was very exciting to go through the creative process that they had used to rebrand numerous other global clients. The very creative and talented people at this firm put together a professional plan with the logo and all of the other products such as letterhead and stationary. The library commissioners approved the plan, and the FOL funded much of the cost of the change over to the new image. It was clear that one of the reasons that it was accepted was the fact that it was created by an ad agency that was headed by a community icon that was well respected for his talent in his agency. The library's new image became well known in the community. Since the library later changed to a new image emphasizing the new main library (NML), little evidence remains of the look it had during the 1990s.

To understand branding, analyze the advertisements for major brands. Much of the time they aren't selling anything new. Most of the TV beer commercials are aimed at being clever or funny and then just displaying the brand. Coke, Pepsi, Budweiser, and on and on are household names. People need to have a positive response to the brand of the library.

Advocacy

Advocacy is often used to describe as an activity for a specific campaign or fund drive and while there are overlapping elements with marketing and branding, the crux of advocacy is the involvement of many volunteers. This can be an outstanding strategy for dealing with political issues and government funding. Having a cadre of leaders for the volunteers that are educated in the issues of the library and its needs for funding is critical. The ability to generate crowds at budget hearings, piles of letters and e-mails to congress, and to have people spread out throughout the community is often the most effective element of library advocacy. It is often stated in fundraising that people donate most to people that they know. Thus, having a lot of advocates is a real plus for fundraising.

Advocacy is more like missionary work than marketing. You are educating and inspiring others to do the communication and to spread the support for the library. Working through others may create situations where you have less control over the message but multiplying the number of advocates is very important.

Within the last five years, the strategy of creating local, regional, and national advocacy programs has moved to the top priorities of library associations and library support groups throughout the United States. Some of the programs are very generic and broad ranging and are designed to support long-term stakeholder creation, community communications, campaigns for specific projects, and advocacy to elected and appointed officials. Some of them are more focused on specific activities such as book sales. ALA's Web site (http://www.ala.org/ala/issues/issuesadvocacy.htm) is a good place to start with.

FOLUSA is another great place for serious resources and support for you and your library. Some of the programs include very specific tools that are targeted to audiences. A brochure that describes advocacy programs by FOLUSA is available at http://www.folusa.org/membership/printable-forms/all-in-one-form.pdf. An example of the program of a workshop conducted by the director of FOLUSA for a state association is at available http://www.sls.lib.ia.us/calendar/folusa. A great introduction to advocacy for library trustees in a PowerPoint presentation is available at http://www.slideshare.net/scstatelibrary/library-advocacy-resources/. The focus on advocacy through the merger of FOLUSA and ALA will greatly benefit the libraries and librarians. Their combined talent and communications skills will be a big boost to the effort to raise the level of support for libraries in this country.

Libraries for the Future, a nonprofit organization that supports innovation and investment in America's libraries, was founded in 1992. They operate programs in more than 220 libraries in twenty-seven states. They usually work in partnerships with libraries, library systems, foundations, and community-based organizations. They currently have a grant from the Bill and Melinda Gates Foundation that has funded the creation of publications to help advocates for libraries. They are accessible at http://www.americansforlibraries.org/.

Many postings on blogs, organization Web sites, and library Web sites ponder this question of how best to ensure that libraries will not only survive, but also thrive. An interesting muse is at http://www.infomotions.com/musings/marketing/ where Eric Lease Morgan presents his thoughts on the issue. The International Federation of Library Associations (IFLA) provides access to a number of papers that have been presented at their conferences. A recent example is at http://www.ifla.org/VII/s40/pub/advocacy-e.htm. This particular paper seems to be most interested in advocacy for libraries with elected officials at the national levels but the range of the papers is from local to international. The creativity of library supporters that is showcased at national and international conferences is very impressive.

Online Computer Library Center (OCLC) has added their significant marketing and communication resources to the effort for library advocacy. Their site at http://www.oclc.org/advocacy/default.htm is a good starting point. WebJunction which is an OCLC program with significant funding by the Bill and Melinda Gates Foundation has a number of tools, tips, discussion, and other helpful information on their Web site at http://webjunction.org/do/Navigation;jsessionid=BFEA459A2967C480D69A51D10DAA6E41?category=405. The list of articles includes presentations on such topics as "Getting on Your Community's Leadership Team," "Building Partnerships Success Stories, and Getting a Seat at the Table." WebJunction is an online community of librarians, library staff, library advocates, and others involved in libraries. It has very robust activities and should be consulted regularly. They presented the Public Library Association (PLA) 2008 Virtual Conference as an extension of the in person conference in Minneapolis.

Be sure and check with your state library association for the local emphasis on advocacy. Much of the money from ALA, OCLC, and other national organizations is provided for the development of state or local advocacy programs. An example of a statewide program can be found on the Web page of the Illinois Library Association at http://www.ila.org/advocacy/advocacy.htm. There is a very active Web site for school libraries in New York at http://www.crbsls.org/slsa/. The Internet Public Library provides links to a number of resources on library advocacy at http://www.ipl.org/div/subject/browse/hum45.20.00/.

Even library vendors that make their money off goods and services to libraries are offering tools and advice for advocacy. ProQuest is a good example, and can be accessed at http://www.proquest.com/division/libraryadvocacy.shtml.

As one might expect, there is a lot of linkages among the Web sites of various organizations. For example, the California Library Association has information on advocacy that links to the ALA Handbook on Advocacy (http://www.cla-net.org/legislation/libraryadvocacy.php). This is a good example of the networking abilities of the Internet and the Web World.

It is not difficult to find information, programs, advice, strategy, nor collaboration for library advocacy. The big challenge (as it often is in the information business) is to focus the information that abounds into knowledge that can be applied to your situation. Assess, streamline, and apply are the three keys to creating an advocacy program. A strong advocacy program is the best long-term strategy for creating and sustaining a library development program. If the library is entering a new era of growth, expansion, and improvement, the advocacy program should be developed early in the strategic planning and community communications program. Your program should be organic. That is in the sense that communications is a two-way street. You should be listening to your advocates as well as educating and inspiring them. What you hear should be included into your planning, services, and development strategy.

Media Storm Firefighting

Today libraries and librarians have their highest profile in history and even though we make an entertaining stereotype based on traditional public perceptions, librarians today are now recognized as community resources more than at any other time. The recent ALA and OCLC public opinion surveys show a high level of regard for libraries and librarians today. While we are still responsible for the traditional functions of the library within the "historical compact," we are now creators and keepers of a robust public domain for communication, creators of community information commons, protectors of fair use, and protectors of first use rights. We also oppose censorship and governmental control over what the public can read, hear, and view with our time and our dollars. While these topics are often controversial, they do provide a topic for conversation that will give the library advocate the opportunity to show that the library is for the common good. It is important that the entire organization and supporters are knowledgeable about these issues and the library's policy concerning them.

Presenters need to be prepared to respond to the issue of the day. They may have been invited to speak about the library but they may also be asked about the Internet filtering, censorship of books, or need for more services. Sometimes, it seems that all of the news media is focused on the library and while that is usually a positive situation for the library there can be some times when the media is focusing on issues that create controversy in the community's perception of the library. At these times, it is very helpful to have some guidance about how to handle the media. SFPL found itself in a storm of controversy in late 1996 and the foundation funded a workshop for the Go-to-Team in how to deal with the news media.

Scott Shafer, a public relations guru in San Francisco who is presently on the staff at KQED, presented a workshop on dealing with the media during crises (Shafer, 1996). He presented something called the "Interviewee's Bill of Rights" that was very helpful. Scott suggests that there are several things to keep in mind while dealing with the news media, particularly in a controversy. For example, you do not have to respond right away, but be mindful of their deadline. "I don't know the answer to that. I'll have to get back to you." Remember though that if you wait too long the story will be written and your view will be left out or made up by someone else. You can ask about the context of the story to get some sense of where the reporter might be biased. You can always use notes, especially if you are on the phone. Ask who else they have talked to (they won't necessarily tell you) and you can suggest people they should talk with. If possible, always send them backup information that illustrates your point. You can ask to be off the record or on background but don't believe for a second that it is 100 percent certain that it will be the case. With electronic media, you can ask them to let you to stop in the middle of sentence and start over if you feel the need. They can edit it out unless it is live on the air. You can ask them to read back your comments, or what they are writing (to some degree). You can say, "This is really very complicated and sensitive and it's important that you understand what I mean." In worst case scenarios, you can call the city editor or news director before the story is filed if you fear the reporter is really going off in a dangerous and misguided direction, but realize that is a desperate act on your part and may pour gasoline on the flames.

When you are dealing in a crisis or near a deadline, get back to them as soon as possible with some information. You should provide them with at least enough for them to make their filing, especially for the radio, and get your point across. You need to try to stay on top of the information and try to keep them on your message, not theirs. It is usually best not to appear to be avoiding them and your stating that you "have no comment" is usually a bad idea. If at all possible, know what you want to say ahead of time and write it down if it will make you more comfortable. Watch out for humor or sarcasm since it doesn't always translate through to the reader, listener, or viewer. This is especially true if it is presented out of context. Don't use jargon that the reader or viewer won't understand.

While your library should have a single spokesperson who is authorized to speak for the library, others in leadership positions should be aware of how to deal with controversial issues whenever possible and they should know as much about the situation as possible. Of course, there are often conflicting viewpoints within an organization and it is difficult to get the media to focus on the organization's view when there are a bunch of people clamoring for attention in the library.

Testimonials

One of the most powerful communication elements is the personal testimonial. These can be very motivating for the person giving the message and motivating for the people receiving the message. Throughout the state of California, there is a strong network of local programs for adult literacy. Many of them are located in the local public library. You can learn about using testimonials from your local Right to Read programs who have mastered the technique.

Testimonials for the NML fundraising campaign were, and still are, very powerful. Almost half of the capital campaign for the NML was raised through the creation of groups who had a special interest in being involved and supportive of the library. They ranged from for the Gay/Lesbians, the African/Americans, the Latino/Americans, to the environmental supporters. Bailey quotes a number of the leaders of the affinity groups for the SFPL NML fundraising campaign. Each of the leaders of the affinity groups had their own testimonials about how important this campaign was to them and their community. The interesting part was that none of them talked about their love of the library and the joys of going to the library as a child. We had many donors and leaders who did remember these times but the affinity groups were not the traditional library users and supporters. The cochairs of the African-American group often stated, "This is the first time the African-American community had been brought in at the beginning, and asked to play a key role. Usually, by the time the black community hears about a philanthropic project the train has left the station." He added, "If we're lucky, we may catch the caboose. At the library, we are riding first-class, and we are paying our way." A leader in the Latino-Hispanic community liked to say, "This campaign is not about money. It's about building community." The library foundation members basically said, "We recognize you should be a part of this, because you are a part of San Francisco. Now, how would you like to participate?" (Bailey, 1994).

You will need to design your own fundraising approaches. Often a group may never have been asked to be a part of any fundraising, and they will be pleased to join. When the foundation asked two prominent leaders and activists in the gay and lesbian community to raise money for the Gay and Lesbian Center, one of their leaders was astonished. He could not recall another occasion on which they had been asked to be part of a mainstream civic project. There were similar responses from the other communities. They were pleased to be asked, got organized, and enthusiastically raised the money. Each group was rewarded not only with their celebration center in the NML but with a party just prior to opening to invite all of their supporters and members of their community.

The underlying point is that these communities in the city had never felt to be a part of the library. While they had used the library and some of them were great supporters, the establishment of the affinity groups gave them leadership opportunities in their own community as well as participation in the project. The outcome was a building that values their diversity, yet provides shared spaces and services for everybody. It was made clear from the start that of the monies raised by the affinity groups one half would go to their special celebration centers and one half would go to common space enhancements.

Anecdotes

One of the other styles of communication is the anecdote. A visiting library director called and asked if she could visit and get a tour. When she arrived at our office she was bursting with enthusiasm, "I asked the taxi driver at the airport if he knew where the new library was and he turned to me and slowly said that he certainly did because he had $50 in that building." It was quite impressive when the library could point out that a million people used that NML in its first six months of operation and that in a year more people used the library than attended all of the professional sports venues in the bay area.

Rethinking Your Look

Media that has been around for at least thirty years is old media. This includes communication vehicles that you can totally control such as flyers, bookmarks, and posters. These items should not be overlooked although the risk is that the public is often bombarded with too many messages when they enter a busy library. These do need to be individualized or focused if possible. Even common presence in the community by the library can be used to send a message.

A bookmobile, for example, may often be the only positive presence of governmental service in a rural area or impoverished neighborhood. Residents in these areas may most think of the county as law enforcement or regulations that control what they can do. A bookmobile can be targeted to specific functions, age groups, and neighborhoods. They get around. A lively, well informed staff on board not only provide good service, they can spread the message. They need to know what that message is however. The branch libraries, outreach centers, and main libraries should be viewed as communication opportunities as well. The buildings themselves convey a message. A drab, uninviting building sends a message the opposite of a bright cheerful one.

Dealing with the News Media

If you can obtain communication channels that go directly to the community without intermediaries or reinterpreters you should take them. A communication channel can be as mundane as a weekly book review or report on library activities or it can be a Cable Television systems (CATV) channel. The local print media is a good way to get started. Neighborhood or small give away newspapers are always looking for free material. It is also a place for your Community Relations Office (CRO) staff to start honing their craft. The local newspapers always need copy of local interest and if it is well written, of interest to readers, and delivered to their deadline they will put it in the paper. Announcements about programs and events will usually be put in the paper. The standard vehicle for getting the information to the papers as well as other news media is a press release. Having someone in the organization skilled in the art of creating interesting press releases is very important. The media are usually on a short deadline and don't want to spend time rewriting your release. The press release in advance of an event may lead to press coverage to alert the public to the event and then the paper might have coverage of the event itself.

Almost every community has shopper's handouts and advertising supported newspapers that love to have free and interesting local copy. These are distributed widely at no charge and if you provide them with press releases or storylines they often will run them. You do have to watch out for being in papers with strange bedfellows. These handouts tend to be quite loose in their editorial policy and often end up supporting radical causes and listening to cranks. In their need to get free copy of quasi-news, they often use specious sources or quote people who have an axe to grind.

Local radio and TV stations provide opportunities for community service information. Talk shows are always looking for talent and it is often possible to set up a regular visit or to let them know that you can be on call for short deadline fillers. Sometimes you do have to watch for getting blind sided when they have a story that they want you to participate in, which is focused on some negative topic and you haven't been alerted to the fact that this is what they will be talking about. The broadcast media often will run public service announcements and will usually make a deal for advertising by giving the library cause a break on the price or providing matching air time for nothing. Cable television is often in the same situation.

Use of e-mail for press releases was an early application of online networking and still has value today. Communication can be accomplished quickly and you can often get rapid feedback. It opens up a channel to a reporter or an editor. One key for dealing with the media is to make a list of the modes of communication that each media or editor prefer. Some prefer a letter, personal delivery, e-mail, or even telephone. This probably relates to the personal style of the person receiving the communication, but it can be helpful in encouraging them to read what you send.

Different media operate differently although the aggregation of the media outlets into large, international conglomerates makes them all seem very similar in what they do. This massification and globalization of the news media make it very difficult for a local agency to get coverage in the historical mainstream press without going to extremes in actions or creating some kind of controversy that the editors think will sell papers or attract viewers. This forces the library staff to become serious about creating its own mass communication channels.

Some public librarians instinctively incorporated community communication channels for electronic media quite early. Public libraries started operating public radio stations and public TV stations several decades ago. The Memphis Public Library Information Center still operates WYPL TV-18 and FM 89.3. They started these in the 1970s (http://www.memphislib.org). They also have an excellent Web site.

Since we often find ourselves dealing with the news media and sometimes they operate in the traditional way, we should know what some of the differences among the media are when we are approached by a reporter.

Print

Print is generally more interested in background and the reporters may still have beats that they specialize in. If this is the case you should use every opportunity to educate the reporter, make them comfortable coming to you for information and help them to feel that you are knowledgeable on the subject. This has changed dramatically in the last couple of decades as the media continues to streamline their operations. But, if it is the case it is worthwhile to invest time providing background on issues, providing them with information that could save them time, and in general cultivating a relationship. You do have to be aware that trying too hard to get cozy could backfire if they feel you are over stepping your bounds.

An effective way to ensure distribution to the taxpayers of your message is to use an advertising supplement in you local newspaper(s). The Lexington Public Library's supplement in the Lexington Herald-Leader on November 1, 2005, makes an appealing case for taxpayer support for the library. *All for a nickel* lists all of the services and resources available to the public for only 5 cents per $100 of the properties valuation. The flyer has a map of their service area with the locations of the libraries and an interesting illustrated history of the U.S. nickel coin. A year later they published a one-page handout that listed the estimated value of all of the services and resources showing that the average per capita tax was $42.24 compared to the average per capita value of $175.97. This kind of information makes for good sound bites for all media but having it in the newspaper lends creditability to the numbers.

Sometimes the city or even public utilities will include free inserts in utility bills or other mailings by the city. They usually won't let you advocate a position or issue but they can be helpful in getting out surveys or public service announcements. There are all kinds of free advertising flyers that could include a public service announcement for the library. Often you will find one representative who will package coverage by a TV station, a radio station, a newspaper, flyers, and now Web sites all together. If the media won't donate time or space you should talk to them about a deal. You will have the FOL put up money for a TV spot if they include a radio spot as well. Maybe they will pay for the production costs. It never hurts to try to get a deal.

Television

Television needs pictures and a thought in less than twelve seconds. When you watch a news show; count how many stories they cover per minute. It is pretty amazing. If you are on camera, you look best if you have some spark. Watch the newscasters or weather persons. Move your hands, smile, nod agreement, and other small motions. Practice the setting before you go to the studio or set up for the reporter. Try to make sure you are in a place where you are comfortable. Hopefully, you won't be confronted by reporters when you are going from one place to another. If you are caught off guard, try to get them to come to your office.

Radio

With radio you must be clear, concise, and use good adjectives or metaphors. You can't use pictures or printed words to enhance. You should make a list of questions that might come up and develop answers that you can have at the ready. Since the audience can't see you it is possible to use notes.

CATV

You should explore access to TV programs on your local Cable Television Systems (CATV). They have certain obligations for community programming and are usually very agreeable to putting quality and informative content on their programs. They may even allow you to operate one or more channels if they have excess capacity. Some library CATV programs have been very effective in getting community support. If you are going to do CATV programs, you must create CATV quality studio facilities and this could be a reason for raising funds. While these libraries aren't always capable of direct broadcast over the network, they need the ability to capture quality video programming. Their ability to capture programming held in the library for archival and dissemination purposes and can be important in constituency building. You might create a series of programs around the early pioneers and important leaders in your community. These productions should be first class and should be an outstanding addition to the local history collection. In addition, they will provide an opportunity for library staff to market the library to your community and enlist the support of the people interviewed.

Since most CATV operations are part of a governmental franchise by a city or county government, you could volunteer to serve on the franchisor's oversight committee or local production volunteers to get a better understanding of how to get your programs on the cable.

TOOLKIT WITH THE NEWS MEDIA

While print, TV, radio, and CATV are still viable communications channels for libraries, the Internet provides opportunities not even imagined decades ago. If you have mastered print and personal messages you have a good start for disseminating your message in new media. While the basic message must be the same, you should use the new capabilities to target audiences and to spread your reach. The variety of new media available to libraries for communication with stakeholders is astounding. They include Web sites, Listserves, e-mail, BLOGS, WIKIS, Flickr, Mashups, MySpace, video casting, and podcasting. There is a good presentation on these and other tools at http://wikis.ala.org/emergingleaders/index.php/List_of_Tools#Blogger.

Avatars in Second Life are a way to create a new you. Bob Mason contends that Second Life gives people the opportunity to create social networks in the way that young children figure out what works and what doesn't work (Mason and Hart, 2007). A baby tries something and if it works the baby's brain will remember the pattern. If it doesn't work they will try something else. This is the process that creates the links in the small brain. It will be interesting to follow this development in the virtual world. It can certainly appeal to the millennium generation who don't have any idea what the world was like before the Internet.

The Alliance Library Network defines Second Life as a 3-D virtual world entirely built and owned by its residents, including real life librarians on Info Island. Spend some time exploring the alliance's Web site (Alliance Regional Library System Second Life). This system also provides opportunities for library users and supporters to get outside training for advocacy. Check it out. The Alliance also allows discounted group rates to members for purchasing security software from Symantec. Their outstanding Web site also lists the unofficial election results or library referenda. This site is constantly updated. For this year they show that five of the seven issues voted on passed. The outstanding communications program of the Alliance such as their presentation about the Illinois Advocacy Day helps the member libraries to have a winning percentage at the polls (Alliance Library System Advocacy Training). They also provide workshops on new information technology such as the virtual world of Second Life (Alliance Second Life).

You will find a tremendous amount of information on it. Their definition of themselves is very clever. It states, "ALS is Amazon, FedEx, a community college, My-space and a potluck dinner all in one." You can join Second Life with a little help from a techno youth. In 2007 the Alliance Library System was cited for leadership and achievement by the Association of Specialized and Cooperative Libraries Agencies, a division of the ALA.

A recent online handbook from the University of California, Los Angeles (UCLA) Libraries Web site lists the steps to produce a podcast (http://www.oid.ucla.edu/units/tec/tectutorials/casting). It looks surprisingly like the methodology that we used to produce story hours on CATV in 1973. A recent graduate of the San Jose State University's (SJSU) School of Library and Information Science (SLIS) program has created a Web site that explores podcasting and provides some hints for a successful program.

ALA and other library organizations are also joining into Second Life. The SLIS at SJSU opened up a space for instructional purposes. Second Life appears to have promise in education although it isn't mainstreamed yet (Second Life Wiki). My-space and other virtual communities have offerings that appeal to the gaming generation and thus have a huge potential for virtual community building among the youth. Virtual fundraising has a great deal of promise to make the funding base identical to the user base but it will remain to be seen if libraries figure out how to do that effectively. The ALA Office for Information Technology provides an excellent overview of social networking (ALA, OITP).

It is also advisable for the library to produce and make available trailing edge technology products such as a DVD or CD that can be distributed on request or simply handed out at various stakeholder events. They are also good as support for presentations made by staff and supporters.

Regardless of the technology used to communicate with the community and stakeholders, there must be a clear consistent message. The clearer and simpler the mission, vision, goals for the library, and the case statement for increased funding are, the better the chances for success are.

While there are many tools there seems to be a lack of strategic focus for all of these tools in most of the library Web sites and in the Internet. They often are built from the bottom up with the focus on the tool acquisition and its implementation without taking the view that the purpose of these tools are for systematic and comprehensive communication. It is great that these tools can be targeted to attract specific stakeholders or groups but the overall look and navigation should be systemic. A look at many existing library Web sites shows that there is a need for a strategic approach that conveys a common message around the mission and vision of the library, updates the viewer on the progress on the plans, and ensures that the library gets credit for all of the marvelous programs and projects.

It is very important that the process for managing and developing the Internet presence is done by someone at the high administrative level. They should be included in all of the discussions with the CRO and represented in the Go-to-Team so that the Internet perspective is the starting point for PR, not a paste-on to the traditional methodologies.

It is important to remember that while they add to the WOW factor of the library, they need to move beyond the novelty into the toolbox of the library. MyLibrary is a concept that people can understand since many Web sites such as Yahoo already use it. It can be personalized without a great deal of effort by the library. Once the software is in place, the user makes decisions for communication and priorities for their personal service and fills out the forms with their basic information and preferences. It can meet the need for the library's communication system to be "Web centric" as discussed earlier.

FINDING COOKBOOKS

Some of the most important tools in the kitchen are the cookbooks. For cooking there are around 1,600,000 hits on the term cookbook according to Google, the bible of information today. For library development there are only 709,000, which is still a lot of sources. This is up from 66,7000 only six months ago. My point is that as with cookbooks you couldn't nor shouldn't expect to buy them all. You only need a few good ones.

FUNDRAISING AND DEVELOPMENT

Many cookbooks on fundraising and development are available. A Google search brings up 39,900,000 hits. The first URL that came up on library fundraising and development is very interesting. Tony Poderis has a site labeled "Fund–Raising Forum." It is an excellent place to start because it is comprehensive, his credentials are impeccable, and all the stuff is free. It is in seven languages and you can even ask him questions via the form provided (http://www.raise-funds.com/).

ALA is a good source for information on fundraising and development for libraries. Their Web site provides a bibliography on consultants which include those for fundraising. The Library Administration and Management Association (LAMA) fundraising and financial development section site is good and includes a moderated discussion (LAMA, FRFDS). The PLA publication with a somewhat lengthy title of Libraries Prosper with Passion, Purpose and Persuasion: A PLA Toolkit for Success can be ordered online at the PLA Web site. It provides a good overview of the strategy and includes nearly 100 pages of step-by-step instruction in a binder and a CD-ROM (PLA TOOLKIT). The New York Library Association (NYLA) has a good Web site on funding development for libraries (http://www.nyla.org). OCLC provides tools on their Web site as does WebJunction.

ALA's executive director of the International Relations Committee, Michael Dowling, made a presentation on advocacy at the IFLA 2007 conference which is available in their proceedings on their Web site (www.ifla.org).

ALA's and other professional associations' Web sites also provide current terminology, definitions, and suggest examples of libraries that have gone through the operationalization of these new technology tools. The point here is that communication for development should be considered a priority for you and a constant assessment of the potential for new tools must be ongoing.

HAPPY COOKING

Now that we have become personally organized, cleaned out the kitchen, and obtained good tools including cookbooks we can start cooking.

5

Nibbles and Starter Recipes

Let's start with nibbles in order to set the stage for major developments such as voter initiatives. It is important that the public perceive the library staff as being good stewards of their money, operating efficiently and effectively, and managing fundraising in a way that reassures the donors and taxpayers that their money is being well spent. Your ability to raise small amounts of money will help build creditability, give the staff and supporters experience in the endeavor, and hopefully, these events will provide a service or experience that the community will enjoy.

Sometimes you may have to use these kinds of fundraising activities to keep the doors open or new books flowing in. In these situations, the case is made for community help because funding has decreased or the city isn't providing adequate funding. These activities can be important not only to get the money restored, but as opportunities to involve many more stakeholders in advocacy. This is the added value of the smaller fundraisers.

Funding for growth requires a departure from the "appeal for the poor library" syndrome which may help to keep the door open from time to time but rarely goes beyond the status quo in development. By embarking on a program of smaller fundraising activities to grow the library's program, you can prepare, execute, and practice fundraising on a small scale. The carrying out of these smaller efforts successfully will support the strategic effort through training of staff and supporters, enlisting volunteers, organizing the effort, and providing seed money for larger fund drives. The money can be used to hire expertise in fundraising and provide talent and energy for the bigger campaigns. When activities such as book sales create new stakeholders and generate support, they extend beyond the short-term goal and strengthen the whole long-term development program.

You have to start someplace and maybe going for a home run on your first time out isn't the best idea. It takes practice to figure out successful fundraising, and it is best to start small. Failure doesn't necessarily prohibit you from trying again and succeeding, but politicians and voters tend to support successful events or issues more than ones that have failed. You and your staff need to learn how to present the case for the funds, how to manage the program, and how to build momentum for strategic development. Start with some of the historic, tried and true activities as a learning exercise. Excellent guidance is available in published literature covering how libraries have been successful with starter activities. Check out the American Library Association (ALA) Web site for starters. You can start with these small recipes.

It is important to have your policies and procedures for all donations whether money or collection items clear and comprehensive. If such policies and procedures are not in place, the gift may be lost. The San Francisco Public Library (SFPL) nearly lost the core of their outstanding calligraphy collection when an heir to the donor requested the return of all the items located in the library that were provided by his father. While the staff of the special collections department was sure that the collector intended to donate the items to the collection, it turned out there was no written agreement or acknowledgment of a gift of the items. The city attorney had to come to the library's rescue. Without this support, the Harrison Collection of Calligraphy and Lettering would just be a footnote in the history of SFPL. Having legal assistance in the development of policies and procedures means the documents will cover the agreements necessary for the gift to be given to the library.

COMMUNITY ORGANIZATION PRESENTATIONS

Practically every community has a host of neighborhood, service, religious, and other clubs that invite guest speakers for their lunches, dinners, and other social events. This presents an excellent opportunity for you to tell your story. Build a brief message around you and your library and ask for their support. You might find a particular area for a specific club. For example, a Toastmasters club might donate money for books on debate or public speaking. The Rotary Clubs are very proud of their international affiliations.

You set a goal for a certain number of presentations on a regular basis, such as three a week, so you can build up your network for when you have a big goal like budget time or a bond issue campaign. Sometimes you will find clubs that don't buy into your message, but often some people will come up after the event and identify themselves as interested in your program.

Start out small, practice, and then train your staff and other supporters to get out the message, too. Let the organizations know that you or a member of your staff is very interested in visiting them, and get going. You can be surprised how a visit to a service club may result in an offer to help through money or volunteers.

While it would appear that the main goal of these nibbles is to raise money, they have other benefits. They can get the staff and supporters used to the idea that the library can and should do events to raise money. It gives the staff and volunteers practice at putting together and operating these events. After a few experiences, a routine will develop and people will be knowledgeable in their tasks. Routines should be documented for future reference and training. They often lead to much bigger development activities. For example, once you start with service clubs in a large city, you must be prepared to appear or have a representative available whenever invited. This may involve many presentations in a year, and if this is the case you should have a roster of staff members, FOL, and other supporters who can help cover the requests. Even in a smaller city, the number of requests may exceed your ability to do each one yourself, and you need to have others available. An added advantage is that this also provides the opportunity for you to expand the knowledge about the library for the library's representative. When you have these persons, you need to give them the assistance they need to be successful.

Orient, update regularly and provide them with audiovisual support tools such as a DVD or a video. Target the speaker to the audience if at all possible. For example, send your board member who is active in the chamber of commerce to speak at their events. Be prepared to take the equipment if, when booking the presentation, the person doing the hosting indicates that they don't have the equipment. Be prepared for fall-back positions as well.

If the audiovisual or online part doesn't work, have a script or notes ready for you to follow. It can be very effective to have a good audiovisual presentation but try the equipment in advance.

These community organization presentations increase the number of stakeholders and should contribute to the creation of a stakeholder communication network. They also give you and fellow presenters a chance to polish your act in preparation for bigger events. These smaller amounts of funds raised should contribute to the ability to increase the promotion, education, and advocacy of the library throughout the community. Remember to leverage these funds.

One of this author's students, a school media specialist, wanted to start a computer lab for her students but the administration would not budget the funds. She took this advice and went to the local parent–teacher association (PTA) to ask for the money for two computers, monitors, and other equipment. She had put together a short but impressive case statement of the need and the PTA was happy to provide the seed money. When she implemented the lab with the two computers, the word spread through the school and the district. The district administration was impressed; and eventually that small donation by the PTA developed into a district-wide computer literacy program with the student as the director of the program.

BOOK SALES

Many times funds are raised where the public receives something in return as well as helping the library. Book sales or donations to the book funds with recognition in a memorial bookplate are good examples. The donor has an individualized and tangible recognition for the money as well as helping the library.

Through local booksales you can get rid of outdated books, copies of books that are no longer popular, and books that haven't circulated for years. A good booksale that is attended by the community is a great idea for recycling the books. This usually appeases people who are aghast at the idea of a library throwing away books since they see them being recycled in the community, and they even have the opportunity to rescue their favorite book if it is in the sale. You do need to develop your spiel to explain to people why this particular book was discarded or not added to the collection.

In large libraries these can number in the tens of thousands each year. None of us likes to throw away any book, yet it is important to keep the collection alive. A relevant, current, authenticated collection is still important in this age of the Internet.

Most of the work for the sale can be done by volunteers. You will need to have an easily accessible place to collect and store the books until the sale, and some sort of organization of them is necessary prior to the sale opening. An informal grouping of the books by subject, age level, and type of fiction facilitates people finding what they want. At the least they should be sorted into children's books, fiction, nonfiction, and biography. Someone from the staff should have at least looked at the books before the sale starts to double check for ones that might be relevant to the collection. You can turn it over to your Friends of the Library (FOL).

Sometimes when the FOL are sorting out the books for their book sale there will be books that appear to be valuable but aren't suitable for the library's collection. Your FOL could offer these through silent auctions during the booksale. Silent auctions and the booksale in general attracted a horde of collectors and dealers who are willing to pay more than the normal price for the regular books in the sale.

Sometimes a group of libraries will coordinate the timing and publicity to spread the reach and access to people seeking booksales. The Wyoming State Library coordinates publicity for booksales throughout the state (Wyoming Library Roundup). The statewide view increases the ability of each individual sale to be successful.

It is now possible to have a continuous and global book sale through the Internet through vendors who sell discards from libraries online and specialize in doing it. One source is at http://Betterworldbooks.com. Amazon and Barnes and Noble will sell library discards as well. While it is an efficient way to raise money, it has less overall value than an actual local book sale event since there is no community connection and little ability to increase stakeholders.

Take a look at other library booksale operations. You can find a good example of an excellent Web site on a booksale from the Zelienople (Pennsylvania) Area Public Library http://www.post-gazette.com/pg/05132/502776.stm.

SPONSORED BOOK FAIRS

Scholastic Books, Inc. often sponsors book fairs featuring their publications for schools and small libraries. You will need to handle the promotions, and you need some space and help with the sales during the event. Some of the proceeds of the sale of books can be provided to the FOL or the PTA for their support of the library.

You may want to consider working with local bookstores or other book-related programs such as Great Books as well. Local bookstores will often provide copies for author programs at the library and give the library part of the proceeds of the sale. The bookstores and other similar businesses should be brought into the stakeholder tent. People who like bookstores also like libraries, and both compliment each other in terms of getting people to read and value books.

COOKBOOKS

The St Mary's County, Maryland library has published and sells a cookbook that includes 300 years of cooking by African American tradition. It is a good seller with over 1,200 copies sold last year. They made $6,000 profit that is used to support public programming (St. Mary's, 2007).

NAMING OPPORTUNITIES

It is common today to raise funds by providing memorial opportunities for a person with recognition plates or plaques in books, on sidewalk pavers, and on areas in a building. Opportunities for corporate donors for programs or physical items are also quite common. The company gets not only recognition by the public and support for a good cause but also a tax deduction. An active library has a host of choices; but there are critics. Donor-contributed funding is still controversial due to concerns that the donors might want to control the library based on the fact that they donated to the library. The library needs to have a written agreement with all donors that clearly spells out expectations and obligations of both sides of the deal with some sense of an appropriate amount related to the benefit to the donor. A new library building would require a major donation in order to be considered appropriate.

All new or renovated buildings provide a plethora of opportunities for funding memorials. If you are just improving the landscaping in an area, a tasteful plaque can provide recognition for donors. Bricks in memory of people can be used to make a pathway or edge to the landscaping. Funding for public computers or new equipment for public service can be acquired from donors in return for recognition. Of course, one must pay attention to the cost for maintenance and eventual replacement. Once these services are started, it is difficult to stop them in a way that doesn't alienate the users of those services.

Bookplates

Recognizing individuals or groups by putting plates into books that have been purchased through donations has been around for a very long time. You can facilitate and market these by providing a wish list for new books in writing or online. This is probably the easiest and most used program in libraries to raise money for collections. It can be effective for one book, a group of books, or an entire collection. Most people feel good if they help to purchase a book for the entire community and get to memorialize someone in the process. You should retain the right to make the selection so that this does not become a way for people to provide a bias to the collection and the standard selection criteria should apply. This is particularly true when the possibility of one part of the collection is overwhelmed by donors of books. Sometimes persons representing a particular religious, political, or group belief that has avid supporters will use a library's willingness to take donations as a way to influence or indoctrinate people. The donors certainly can make suggestions or request a specific book but they should be advised that normal collection standards apply.

Create an attractive bookplate that should be coordinated with the look of other public relations material. A standing procedure should be set up and tasteful advertising of the opportunities should be presented. All public service staff should know of this opportunity and be encouraged to suggest it to people with whom they interact. At least one public library, the Boulder Colorado Public Library, has printed a list of titles desired for purchase and urges people to donate funds for purchase of these books. The Oakland Public Library created a wish list on Amazon.com. This is a perfect application for online funding support solicitation which we will explore in context of the MyLibrary design.

Donated Subscriptions

Some libraries have programs where staff members solicit individuals or businesses to support the purchase of magazines. The plastic binders in which the magazine is displayed can show the name of the donor. This kind of program must be managed and assessed so that the public does not feel that the library is overzealous in its fundraising and it should ensure that the returns exceed the cost of doing the program.

Like other funding "asks," the staff should be knowledgeable in why the donations are needed, should be motivated as salespersons for the whole library program, and should be diplomatic and enthusiastic about what they are doing. It should be remembered however, that often the cost of the employee time getting a subscription may be more than the cost of the subscription and once a subscription is started the users tend to expect it to continue even though the library budget is inadequate to cover its continuing.

SERVICE OR PRODUCT DONATIONS

Another opportunity for support can be in the form of services or donated equipment. For example, caterers or restaurants can donate food service for library functions in return for recognition. In building a new library in San Francisco, one prominent coffee shop corporation was contacted because the architects wanted to use a plastering process developed several centuries ago in Venice. This process used coffee as the coloring in the plaster used to finish walls. Since the library's atrium and much of the interior of the building was to be plastered a lot of coffee was needed. This simple request resulted in an excellent collaboration to make a better library. The supplier went on and provided free coffee service to many library functions for several years. All of these opportunities must be managed strategically with a clear understanding by both parties of policies and procedures.

PUBLIC PROGRAMMING

Offering programs of interest to the public is an excellent way to attract new users, connect with existing users, and create good will on behalf of the library. They also provide opportunities for creating new partners in your community that will expand the ability of the library to provide programs and services. Programming can be segmented to focus on different audiences. For those who like to travel or who would like to travel, a travelogue program is of interest. Talks by authors of books can draw a crowd.

It is obvious that the more publicity there is the more people are likely to attend. What is often not realized is that it takes almost as much effort to advertise a single event as to do a series. The library should have a framework for their programs that puts them in a series. This framework should provide communication opportunities that can be used to schedule events of opportunity when they arise. Establish a pattern, perhaps Wednesdays are the days that your library can telecast a series of events on your local CATV channel. Start with the library's story time for children, work through the FOL Book Program, move to a program in a series on careers, along with other programming to fill the day. You could offer a discussion form and encourage the public to call in and add to the discussion. By organizing your programs in a series, the different news media can publicize your series at the start and then would have the information for every week in front of them. A follow-up expanding on the original information focusing on the next program serves as a reminder that the program is coming up this week.

What you want to do is to create the image in the mind of people that the library is a popular, active, and interesting institution. Sports figures are often made available for programs by their team's public relations people. ALA and the National Football League have worked together to encourage children to read. Storyhours are always popular and some of them are focused on the very young. Lapsit programming for babies is a good way to get the child used to going to the library; it develops the habit for the parent as well and it makes the family aware of the library's needs.

It is important to have goals for the programming. Sometimes the goal is to attract new users, but that may not be the case of who shows up. A series of local history programs using prominent authors may not bring in very many new users but it may lead to active support by history-minded people and their organizations. You should track attendance at events and evaluate them as you go along. If you have a Decision Support System, you should be able to track the usage of the library by the attendees before and after the programs. In one instance Pike's Peak Library District (PPLD) found that while the high-tech programs brought in new people, programs on local history attracted current users more than new ones.

The National Endowment for the Humanities is an excellent source of funding for historical or literary programs. While you must apply for these, when you have a successful program, it will often lead to later grants as well. Keep in mind that it is not a good idea for a public library to charge an admission fee for a public program unless it is very well done and advertised. On the other hand, public programs do provide a good opportunity for grant funding and private sponsorship.

If you survey your patrons about their opinions of what the library is offering, you may find that the highest and best use of library staff is not collection related. You may learn that, while the collections are still important, they alone will not sustain a viable library in the future. The modern library must be multifunctional in its operations and resources. It must be able to meet broader needs of the community and to expand the number and type of stakeholders to remain relevant to the community. The critics of the library that moves beyond the bibliophiles and literary model of library functions and services need to realize that the historic service support is waning.

GOLF TOURNAMENT AND BASEBALL GAMES

The Bellingham Public Library in Massachusetts has an annual golf tournament with the proceeds going to the FOL. The Phoenix, Arizona Public Library has had golf tournaments as well. Another Massachusetts library at Marston Mills raffles off tickets to the Red Socks game with the Yankees. These may not be the source of large amounts of money but they get the libraries favorable publicity, increase the number of stakeholders, and provide fun for the participants.

FEES FOR SERVICES

You may need to consider user fees for some services. You must realize that there may be considerable debate and even opposition for services or programs that have been provided with taxpayer funding. Some people consider a public library as a "free" service with no cost whatsoever. In some libraries there has been consistent opposition to fees of any kind. Often these critics receive considerable coverage in the press since the press sees the issue as controversy. A good argument can be provided by communicating the concept of the historic compact and equity of access as two basic arguments. There is further discussion on this idea in Chapter 7, The Keys to the Financial Castle Kitchen. While the issue is complicated and needs a great deal of consideration (including public input), it should not be dismissed out of hand. The issue is not whether to charge fees but whether it increases access to information and knowledge or diminishing people's access.

On other occasions charging a fee for a service not only makes sense, it serves other purposes than just getting the money. Most libraries that provide photocopying services, either self-service or staff provided, charge a fee. This serves several purposes.

Hopefully, people will copy pages from the book rather than tearing them out or stealing the book. The revenue provides the money to buy the paper and other consumable supplies. Consumption will be capped by the cost to the user. If it were free, some people would use up a lot of supplies and hog the machine. A final effect is that with a charge the library shouldn't be in direct competition with businesses that provide copying services.

It is general practice that people are charged for items not returned. It is often seen as punitive as are overdue fines but their purpose is to provide funds for replacement. It is rare, however, for revenue from fines and lost book fees to actually be placed in the library's budget. Librarians usually have to take them out of their regular book budget.

SMALL COMMUNITY FOUNDATION GRANTS

Most communities have some kind of local community foundation that focuses on improving the quality of life in that community. You may need to search in the National Foundation Directory for them. The nearest foundation center can be a big help. Their directories will indicate the areas that the foundations support. Sometimes a foundation will only support a private entity and if so, it isn't productive to approach them for funding for a public library. Some of them are geographically focused and only fund programs in a specified area. The local ones may provide funds for programming, special services, and some collections. If your region does not have a local foundation center, you may want to partner with a local foundation for funding to the library to become an affiliate of the National Foundation Center and then provide monies to keep the collection updated.

Local foundations are often willing to provide matching funds for other grants. The ability to match funds such as those from Institute for Museums and Library Services (IMLS) is very important. Cultivating a relationship with a local foundation can be well worth your time. Put the director(s) of local foundations on your "must visit" at least once a year list.

PARTNERSHIPS WITH OTHER CULTURAL INSTITUTIONS

Working with other cultural institutions seems logical for libraries, but like all networking activities they take time and need to be assessed for mutual benefits. While it can be an important part of the strategic development program when it opens new doors in the community for the library, sometimes there is competition for the donors of cultural activities. Few incentives were seen for librarians to work with museum directors except for public relations opportunities, some contact development, and the camaraderie of leaders facing similar opportunities and challenges until the IMLS was created. The emergence of the IMLS has created tremendous opportunities for joint programs with funding from the federal government for museums and libraries. The current administration has given priority to funding for IMLS, and it has become a major driver for collaboration among museums and libraries. Their Web site has a ton of information on collaborative activities and funding opportunities. You should understand that funding development is not a "zero sum game" where you have to fight and compete with other agencies or institutions for the same dollars. The better strategy is to work together to increase the size of the pie, rather than fight with your allies and potential allies over the size of the pieces.

PARTNERSHIPS WITH FELLOW GOVERNMENT AGENCIES

Often you might have strange bedfellows and you didn't even know it. The director of a large public library should get close to the leadership and management of its airport. Generally speaking, airports have their own sources of revenue (most of it from the federal government and airlines), and they may be able to get legislation and regulations that prohibit the city from siphoning off any significant proportion of those revenues. Most major airports have exhibit spaces that the library can use to promote the library. You might consider a reading room at the airport. Lots of people are coming and going, and this could be a good promotion opportunity.

CHARITABLE PLANNED GIVING

It is important that you educate your community, stakeholders, and specialists in creating lifetime and estate giving (attorneys and tax specialists) in the need of the library for financial support from individuals and estates. Gifts considered Partnership Gifts include Charitable Remainder Annuity Trust, Charitable Gift Annuity, Charitable Lead Trust, and Charitable Remainder Unitrusts. Some gifts come from estates such as a bequest in a will or a living trust. You need to start with a good case statement as to why the library needs these kinds of support. We will just explore some of them here. A really good introduction is from the Placentia Public Library's Web site http://www.plan.gs/CategoryDetailList.do?orgId=5311&categoryId=208.

Remainder Trusts

Professional fundraisers are very familiar with remainder trusts. You should make sure that your foundation includes this as an option for library support. Basically, they include a provision in a person's will that some of their assets will be donated to the library in their will in return for benefits while they are still living. Many churches rely on these trusts. People can take tax deductions in advance or transfer their property to the library while still living and receive monies from the organization for current living expenses. Once you have it set up, you should make sure that the attorneys in your community know that this option exists by presenting at programs to the local Bar Association.

Wills and Bequests

Some people would like to leave assets to the library in their will. In San Francisco a resident willed a house to the library. No one was aware of this person's intentions. After his death the title of the property was transferred to the library and when sold it added several hundred thousands of dollars to the FOL. It is important for attorneys and individuals to know that donations to the public library should go to the FOL or Library Foundation unless they can specifically target their bequest to the library only. The opportunity for including the library in a person's will should be marketed to attorneys and directly to the users in a tasteful manner. It is advantageous if the library has a procedure that ensures that the local attorneys are familiar with the opportunity for people to contribute to the vision of the library. It should be made known as broadly as possible. In the case of major donations, your attorney should be involved in drawing up the terms if possible. The American Association for Law Libraries has good information for the layperson on the different instruments or strategies for a person to give money to nonprofit organizations (AALL). The Placentia Library is right up front with information, advice, and interactive assistance for charitable planned giving. It is excellent (http://www.placentialibrary.net/library/). In all of these issues it is critical that you have a policy and procedure in advance that allows it to deal with future contingencies and that the library have authority to spend such monies received.

DIRECT MAIL CAMPAIGNS

You will be surprised at the results of a direct mail campaign in your community. If you have a good case statement, a good mailing list, and a well produced piece of literature people will donate. Use professionals who know how to organize it and, depending on the situation, use an automated mailing list.

You can include a section asking for permission to send e-mails to the user and ask if you can send them information on library development at the time that they register for library services. It is O.K. to ask people to donate to the library if they have indicated in their registration form that they are willing to be educated in the needs of the library. It might cause concern if you used the patron registration list for solicitation without the person's prior permission. The same is true on the e-mail listserves. Ask for their permission to send them opportunities to support the library as well as programs that they might be interested in attending.

ENDOWMENTS

Endowments are very difficult in these days of fewer than 5 percent interest. It takes around $2 million to raise $100,000 per year. Because it is so difficult, you should have information and procedures available, but would not give it the highest priority in terms of marketing.

STATE FUNDING

While most states provide grant opportunities or basic budget subsidies out of state funds, they vary widely from state to state. Very few libraries have local funding less than two-thirds of the library's budget. Perhaps the best example of significant state funding for public libraries is in Ohio, which get a major share of their funding from the state.

The states of New York and Illinois also provide significant revenue, but many states provide very little. Be sure and check with your state library and your state library association about the situation. Funds from the state provide a good opportunity for leverage programs since they are usually not treated the same in the local library budget. Projects for planning, community surveys, and other research activities for development can often get funding through sources at the state level.

Public libraries in the states in the northeast tend to have more state subsidy for their operations than in other states. For example, the state of California has very little state funds going to local libraries for operational programs. If library supporters have to decide whether to lobby funds for a state program such as the state library or a program that will benefit their local library, there is a tendency to put their energies into getting funding for the local library. On the other hand, in California the library community has been quite successful in getting state funding to supplement library construction through Bond Act Funding authorized by the legislature and approved by the voters. This has stimulated a large growth in building new or renovated libraries in California today.

Every library, which receives public funding for the state, should be supportive and involved in their state's professional association for libraries. In most cases the most active association at the state level is the one that has programs for all or most of the libraries. A very long time ago a state senator told this author that he wasn't at all interested in supporting local libraries in his state until the librarians in his constituency got their act together. It is difficult to speak with one voice but the more the agreement and common the effort, the greater the chance of success.

Because of the limited numbers of libraries and types of library in a state with as small a population as Wyoming, coordinating a statewide perspective for the libraries there is relatively simple. Wyoming has only twenty-three public libraries (one for each county), twenty-three school district library programs (one for each county), four community college libraries, and one university library. So, all of the public libraries tend to be on the same wave link for statewide programs and it is pretty easy to work with the local school district librarians. The academic libraries view themselves as part of the group as well.

In Colorado the public libraries include city libraries answering to their city, county libraries answering to their county, and regional district libraries answering to two or more local jurisdictions. They all have different legal status and funding sources. Working with the school district libraries is a challenge as well since the jurisdiction of a school district varies from a single city in each county to a countywide district. This lack of common boundaries with public libraries makes it difficult to have joint school/public library programs. Just doing the summer reading program means that the librarians have to approach each school district individually. While the academic libraries often participate in the professional activities, they usually stayed out of any political involvement for libraries in the state.

While the advocacy program for public libraries in California has been quite successful in bringing the public libraries together for common statewide goals, it has not been easy. In California the academic librarians tend to be more involved in the California Association for Research Libraries or their own super institution networks such as the library directors of the California State University system or the University of California system.

The people who you are trying to influence need to be approached in a nonconfrontational situation where they have some time to communicate. These relationships should be cultivated even if there is no campaign underway at the time. It is the relationships that are based on trust or goals that are beneficial to both parties. Persistence is usually critical because trust takes time to develop.

Attention should definitely be paid to opportunities for you to get state funding that can be used to expand their programs or services since they can augment the library's funding base. On the other hand, they should never be taken for granted for long-term continuance since they tend to be targeted for specific programs and for a limited amount of time. The focus is often on start up or demonstration programs. On the other hand these funds can be an excellent source for the planning, research, and establishment of a local campaign to raise local funds. They allow you to do your homework without creating too much of a presence on the political radar screen.

FEDERAL FUNDING

ALA and other professional associations are very active on behalf of library issues before the Congress and the president. The leadership of the ALA Washington Office is considered one of the most trusted advocacy programs by the members of Congress. ALA in cooperation with the District of Columbia Library Association has excellent programs such as the Library Day on Capitol Hill. They also have grass-roots advocacy networks, getting the word out at the right time, and thorough updates for ALA members and all libraries.

The ALA Washington Office has a service providing updates on happenings in Congress and the federal government (ALA Washington Office). The Young Adult Library Service Association (YALSA) and most of the other ALA divisions have blogs and alerting services as well (YALSA blog). YALSA also has a good tip sheet on meeting with your elected officials that makes a lot of sense and increases the effectiveness of visiting a Congress person. ALA's Office for Intellectual Technology Policy in Washington, D.C., provides research and advice to Congress, the president, and other federal officials concerning the impact of technology on access to information and knowledge, advocates for open access and keeps the ALA members informed about activities in the federal government.

In addition to its lobbying efforts, which serve to keep federal funding for libraries in legislation, ALA has an excellent Web site (http://www.ala.org/ala/issues/issuesadvocacy.htm) for locating people, programs, and funding sources for additional funds. The Mid-Hudson Regional Library System has a great Wiki on Grants for libraries in their region (Mid-Hudson).

Don't forget personal communications via your elected officials. When you are applying for a federal or state grant, keep your elected officials in the communication loop. When you get the money, thank them and include them in events for all your stakeholders. When you are doing your "family celebrations" that are discussed in Chapter 7 include your elected officials whenever you can.

INNOVATIVE COMMERCIAL APPROACHES

Credit Card Programs

You can make a deal with credit card companies and provide credit cards just like airlines, banks, and other causes in order to create something new and receive some money. A share of .0001 percent is a lot if your card gets 100 million in business ($10,000). If they use the cards you gain both ways: you get your percent and you may get more fine money since people view charging to a credit card as not as onerous as digging up the cash.

Transit Companies

A good location for marketing information is the local buses, trains, or light rail systems. Although they usually rent the poster space for commercial purposes, they sometimes will allow a city agency or a nonprofit social service to use space that isn't rented. They may also discount their rate significantly and allow you to have two or three ads for the price of one. When you are creating your image pieces, consider all formats ranging from logo to flyers and bus signs. The Louisville Public Library is very creative in negotiating a deal with the local transit company to provide a 50 percent discount for teenagers to ride the buses if they meet their goal of number of books read.

Stay in the Library Forever

Notre Dame University and the University of Richmond have recently joined the group of colleges in the "Back to School...Forever" movement. As reported in the bulletin, a number of colleges have followed the lead of the University of Virginia in the early 1990s which allow alumni and faculty to inter their ashes on school grounds. I am not sure how it would be adapted to libraries but it has really catchy phrases. "If you adored campus life and would die for you alma mater" is pretty classy. For a few thousand dollars you can have your urn placed in a memorial wall or columbarium. College officials are watching to see if the trend, which began at the University of Virginia in the early 1990s and has spread to at least eight other schools, leads to bigger alumni donations. Even if it doesn't, it still puts a new twist on the phrase "hanging around campus" (AARP Bulletin, 2007). This might be a bit far fetched, but it is certainly creative.

Creative Projects with Dedicated Supporters

If the library has built a trustworthy image and presents needs or opportunities for library growth that can enlist stakeholders, there may be many pleasant surprises. A well-known photographer in Colorado Springs was a strong supporter of the library. He documented the culture and history of the community for the Local History Collection. One time he surprised everyone announcing that he would help the library by auctioning off his collection of duplicate photographs. It was held at the local Center for Fine Arts with underwriting by the FOL. They guaranteed that the cost of the event would be paid even if it didn't raise any money. It was a wonderful event allowing many people to buy personally and historically significant photographs. The event raised around $100,000 for the FOL and created a whole new group of stakeholders from the fine arts community.

Another person who should be enlisted as an advocate for the library should be the local public guardian. They have the responsibility of dealing with estates that have no apparent heirs. If there are truly no heirs, the assets of the estate are assigned to a government fund for such purposes. In San Francisco, the public guardian asked for assistance from the library to assess the value of a large collection of printed music. The deceased had been a music dealer with a reputation of being able to provide little known works to musicians and organizations such as a symphony. The guardian did eventually find two nieces who had had little contact with their aunt and little interest in the music. While the library didn't have a budget to purchase the collection, it did have a strong supporter of the music collection program at the library who volunteered to lead the effort to raise the money. He got a musician to give a concert to which the FOL sold tickets and the evening was successful in raising the money for the purchase of the collection.

A long-time supporter of the rare book and fine printing collection worked tirelessly to help the library raise money for this collection. His passion is for classic reprints or printing new classic books and his connections with the antiquarian book dealers and fine printers is a great help to that collection. This supporter provided the introductions for the library staff to become involved in the Antiquarian Book Dealers Association.

At their national conference in San Francisco, library staff was able to demonstrate the library's excellent program with the book arts and with funding from the FOL in a booth displaying the model of the new main library (NML). This created another group of stakeholders.

Your city may be blessed with a number of people that have created outstanding restaurants and have become celebrity chefs. Whether or not they are world famous, they may be willing to support worthy causes through providing fundraising dinners or catering celebrations for donors.

You may be able to get wineries or wine distributors to put on wine tasting events. It is customary for the wineries to host wine tasting for worthy causes. They get the publicity, are associated with a good cause, and seem to enjoy the attention. The tradition may have been started with family-owned wineries but the tradition continues even when they have gone corporate. Wine tasting is a great way to get people together for networking and for the library to create new stakeholders.

Special collections provide enormous opportunities to create supporters. While it is necessary to do homework to identify and pursue people who are passionate about them, it is worth the effort. They can be treasures in and of themselves, but they can also create stakeholders for the library as a whole. For example, at San Francisco Public Library (SFPL) the Robert Grabhorn Collection on the History of Printing and the Development of the Book has value to the digital age innovators. Adobe used the early type style books from this collection when they were creating computer fonts for their software. The same is true for the Richard Harrison Collection of Calligraphy and Lettering. The Schmulowitz Collection of Wit and Humor (SCOWAH) is a good source for comedians, the comedy clubs, and cartoon folks.

When you have special collection strengths, highlight them. The Memphis Public Library has excellent presentation of the drive to fund the music heritage embodied in their special collection on music from Memphis. They provide an excellent statement of the need and challenge the community to support the effort. They make it easy to donate by check in the mail, or person, and online via a credit card.

Be sure to have a procedure to evaluate the "orphan books" that get left donated, sometimes just on the steps of a library. Finding real treasures might take some time; it is not only worth the effort if you find one but it demonstrates to the community that the library still values books.

Raising Money Online

Technology provides tremendous new opportunities for effective communication that can generate support for the library. There are blogs, Ipods, Instant Messaging, Wikis, Google placement, social networking technologies, and many other tools to build communities online (Farkas, Library Success). Farkas is a great source for current participatory information on technology issues. Start with her main page (http://www.libsuccess.org/index.php?title=Main_Page) and work through. She writes and presents often on the topic and makes a lot of sense in her approach. Farkas also points to some great programs that have had successful fundraising programs that maximize the Web presence for donations to the library. This confirms what we already know by our experience in traditional fundraising, that the key to success revolves around presenting a good case for the program, communicating it in a targeted fashion, and creating supportive stakeholders.

In the Library Web site Hall of Fame for academic libraries there are twenty-two listed. Twelve of them have promotions for giving to the library although only a few put them on the home page. Good examples are the Massachusetts Institute of Technology. Listed at "GIVING" on the home page it has extensive follow-up information (http://libraries.mit.edu). Fresno State University has an excellent Web site with a corner cut on giving on the home page (http://www.csufresno.edu/library/). With just a couple of clicks you can get to online giving. Based on the comments of the University President, the University is having an exceptional year for donations. The University of California Los Angeles (UCLA) libraries have an excellent site for giving including online via your credit card. Their list of options is extensive and includes direct gifts, securities, matching gifts, real estate, bequests, charitable gift annuity, materials, and qualified retirement plans. UCLA also will provide you with a library card good at their libraries even if you aren't a student or faculty member if you donate $80 or more. You should be working with experts in dealing with these options. The University of Texas Libraries provides excellent directions for donating online and puts the link right on the home page.

The same survey for libsucess.org shows that of twenty-four public libraries listed as having the best Web sites only thirteen mention giving in their Web site. Of those eight have it on the home page. The Toronto Public Library has an excellent presentation on supporting the goals of the library. The information about the support groups such as the foundation and the Friends is excellent (http://www.tpl.toronto.on.ca). Their choices for support activities include donating online which makes it easy for people to become involved. The mission statements of the library and the foundation are well crafted.

Hennepin County Library is another outstanding example for supporting your library. They also include their privacy policy prominently on the donor page. It would be interesting to track the community relations efforts of the Hennepin County Library with that of the Minneapolis Public Library. Hennepin has been a shining example of success for public libraries for several decades and Minneapolis seemed to be beset by controversy and lack of funding for nearly the same amount of time. Hennepin County library's Web site is a good example of giving the user the opportunity to donate online to support the library, join the Friends, or Foundation, or to volunteer in the library.

While a look at the Minneapolis Public Library Web site shows an impressive array of services, the visibility of development is pretty well buried under program pages such as the FOL. These two systems are now merging. This will certainly spread the tax base, provide different leadership to the library, and perhaps overcome some of the historic dysfunctional aspects of the Minneapolis Public Library.

The Denver Public Library has some interesting wrinkles. Their site lists opportunities for support and provides you the opportunity to buy books through Amazon.com or the local Tattered Cover Book Store and the library sells historical items online. The links to the online books stores provide quite a contrast. Amazon.com pioneered the bookstore that served its customers online and the Tattered Cover Book Store is a legendary local bookstore that has championed intellectual freedom for decades.

The Contra Costa County Library has an online donation form but doesn't get into the planned giving and other arrangements like the Toronto Public Library. The Carnegie Library in Pittsburgh makes it easy as does the Boston Public Library. A survey of these sites and others is instructive as to how effective they are. Even if the funds are donated to the FOL or Foundation, your announcement should be on the front page of the library's Web site so that everyone can see that people are supporting the library all of the time.

Set up special communications paths to donors such as e-mails, e-publications, and even blogs to keep them involved.

Your library may want to partner with someone to do the processing of online donations. The ALA Freedom to Read Foundation uses Give Direct for credit card processing service to handle online donations. It is assumed that part of the reason is to ensure confidence in the process by donors. If you use an external program to manage the process, it should be integrated into the library's Web site architecture. The program should not only communicate support opportunities but include online forms to get the supporters involved and to even make donations. The Web page for donations should be a secure one and should state on the page that it is secure thus giving confidence to folks who might be concerned.

Talking about the incorporation of new technology into the library program is sometimes problematic. Is it a technique, a mindset, a procedure, an opportunity, a cost, a measure of ability, or other category? We are on the cusp of a new era in the use of new technology in libraries. It is all of the above and more, but the most significant element for this book is that it is the single most important new element in fundraising today and holds a great deal of promise. It tracks with the societal trends of the younger generations, is cost effective, and extends opportunities for access to more and more people extensively. The next era will see technology revolutionizing the process for getting the money for libraries for those who understand the value, take the time, and get the resources to build the system. More specific strategy for the development of this system is found in Chapter 7 where the focus is on keys to success.

Now it is time for the big-time stuff. You have completed all of the items on the list up to Chapter 5 and you have done some of the nibbles there. You have raised some seed money and put in to practice the procedures for managing the event from beginning to end. You should have confidence, experience, a good set of supporters, and are ready to expand your development.

In summary, you need to be aware of all of the options for funding in order to create your mixed source funding. It is also important that you should educate yourself on the pitfalls of funding from the different levels as well as the opportunities.

6

Holiday Menus
(Strategies to Get Major Funds)

In looking at libraries in the United States, there is a strong correlation between the ones with the most dynamic and community oriented programs and those that have a mixed source of funds. Total reliance on government funding will often reduce the ability to be innovative, tend to lead to mediocrity, and subject the library to the total control of the funding body and thus the vagaries of political agendas. While few elected officials are opposed to a library and its services, they often have higher priorities that require new funding or restructuring of the library's budget. If your only option for a holiday meal was one dish that's probably what you would have, but your meals would get very boring quickly.

The analogy of a holiday meal, like Thanksgiving in the United States, Christmas for the Christians, Hanukah for the Jewish, Ramadan for Muslims, and celebrations for other groups, is used to create the setting for our funding development program. These celebrations require planning, acquiring the ingredients, having the cooking vessels, recipes for the dishes, timing the meal, serving, and last but not least, the enjoyment of a feast with friends and family. The most successful meal requires planning the menu, getting the ingredients, cooking the food, and enjoying the results.

In the funding world, the major campaign usually takes longer than the annual budget process. It involves many more people (stakeholders), requires a number of years for completion of the goal, and takes seed money to succeed. A really good ingredient for guaranteeing success is to have a knowledgeable, motivated chef who can orchestrate the entire process. That doesn't mean that they have to know everything in the kitchen, but a good knowledge of cooking is important, the ability to bring all of the parts together, and to motivate all involved is paramount.

This chapter will cover how to choose a major marketing campaign including picking a theme, private funding campaigns, corporate or business approaches, and the components of a major campaign using family foundations, community foundations, and affinity groups. It will also show how to use government sources including local, state, and federal funding to prime the process for success. The ultimate will be running campaigns for local referendums, which will be discussed in detail.

The goal of the development program must be based on a vision of the institution in the future. The chance of success is much higher if there is a vision of the future which can be used to inspire stakeholders. This is not too difficult since the institution must change to meet the changes of the community that take place over time. Margaret Knox Goggin, dean of the University of Denver Library School in the 1980s used to paraphrase John Nesbitt and say that "We are in a time of parenthesis. Libraries are in a time of change. We aren't what we were and we aren't what we will be" (Goggin, 1984). It is the vision that must be communicated, not just the need for money.

This is a good perspective for those of us who are pledged to developing libraries. It is not just a phrase but it should be a mantra. In today's world, status quo isn't a viable option. You can go forward or you can go retro but you can't stay the same. If you have done your homework with cleaning out the kitchen, equipping, and organizing, you are ready for the holiday menu. The next step is to identify and articulate the ingredients, your list of needs for funds for implementation of change.

The concept of a recombinant institution sets the table for constant, evolving change. For example, the public library has become a lifeline to the greater world, particularly for those who don't have Internet connections at home. Just find the nearest public library and use theirs. If you are traveling and your laptop is equipped with a wireless connection, you can sit in the parking lot of many public libraries and do your online business. What you will be perhaps amused at is the fact that others are huddled in their cars using the library's WiFi. It is creating a new kind of stakeholder for libraries.

At the 2007 American Library Association (ALA) conference, Andrew A. Venable, Jr., the director of the Cleveland Public Library, was sharing a beautiful twenty-one-page booklet titled *Reinventing Ourselves For You: 2006 Annual Report*. It is colorful, with lots of pictures (especially of kids), contains a great deal of history, and has an excellent vision for the future shown as a case statement document. Its sections are titled: "Reinventing Ourselves For You," "Reading Is for Everyone," "Engaging the Community," "You Spoke. We Listened, We Took Action," "Connecting with Community," "Resources Available to Our Community," "Access to our Resources, How Dollars Were Spent," Planning the Future," and "Behind the Scenes." It is good that it starts out with the future before listing current services and programs. This approach is unusual. http://www.cpl.org/2006-annual-report.pdf.

MARKETING CAMPAIGN THEMES

Having a specific campaign theme, an articulated purpose for fundraising is very important. All, or some of the activities can be used to generate funds but the ability to focus on one theme to specific stakeholders is more effective. For example, if you have a strong group of stakeholders that are most interested in building the collection, you should approach them for assistance in creating collection excellence. The collection that is to be outstanding should be identifiable and have users who understand its value to themselves and the community. A standard practice for private or nonprofit funds a couple of decades ago, it is more difficult now to raise monies for collection development in the Internet era.

Collection Excellence

Perhaps one of the most used themes in the traditional library was the need for more books or printed materials for the collection. The case would be made for either the whole collection being upgraded or specific topics or special collections. It was pretty easy to make the case once you identified the goals for the collections. Most generally the library would approach individuals or funding sources that supported reading in general or specific parts of the collection.

The concept of collection excellence is very narrow now. ALA has done away with standards for collections and the role of collections of books or other print sources has changed. They are still important for a good library but their role is not all encompassing as they were in the days before the Internet and other computer generated sources. A good example is the need to respond to a community of recent immigrants who need to have books and other materials to provide them a link with their historical culture and to help them assimilate into their new community.

Channels beyond the Print Collection

The addition of "channels" (the online, Internet sources) in addition to or in place of collections has changed the library world. This trend will continue to explode as funding sources such as Google and the Gates Foundation continue to pump megabucks into the digitization of content to be available on the Internet. Even the term "channels" is becoming obsolete in our analogies for access to digital content. It seemed applicable when library digital content was mostly online databases available through Lexis/Nexis, Lockheed, and other online database providers. Google isn't exactly a channel. Someone said that the Internet was simply a cloud of users and that still resonates, but now there is more and more content that is peer reviewed or is from an authoritative source.

Funding New Technology

As mentioned earlier, Google has committed huge sums to create new or reformatted digital content and the Gates Foundation is also spending a great deal of money to expand community online technology access through equipment and training in public libraries. State and federal funding is expanding support for digital content and access. Yet, with all this money there is still a need for locally generated government or private funding for the libraries to deal with technology. Most of the stakeholders in libraries see access to the Internet as a valid and important function of libraries. The public seems to have an insatiable appetite for technology in libraries. It is difficult to keep up with the number of access points needed.

When you walk through a library, it is a revelation to note how many users are less likely to be using traditional collections or services vs. those who are on the workstation or laptop. It is startling to go through a historic library that has been recently renovated at the cost of millions of dollars and see that the primary use of the facility is to house the technology for users' access to the online world and the people using it.

Public Programming

We talked about public programming in the previous chapter where we presented it as a starter program that could generate publicity and perhaps some seed money. There is the potential for major fundraising. Many local foundations, corporations, or grants will fund public programming in libraries. While this is probably not a way to raise major funds for capital projects or operating expenses directly, the stakeholders that it can create and the marketing opportunity for a major campaign can be beneficial. Pick an area in which the library has good collections such as local history, special collections, or good contacts for the program talent. Look for partners who have convergent goals. The National Endowment for the Humanities (NEH) is a historic example of partnering with local libraries and library associations such as ALA. At the annual ALA conference in 2007, ALA provided recognition for the NEH public programming funding for libraries. For many years the Friends of the Library (FOL) of the San Francisco Public Library (SFPL) underwrote an annual series of literary programs that usually sold out their tickets. Started more than thirty years ago by, it was a big-time social event and so profitable that the promoter eventually took over the entire program from the FOL. You could try a similar program in your library and check its success.

Age-related programming can also be used to market the library's major campaigns. Young adult (YA) programming is getting the attention it deserves. A great source of information for YA programming can be found at "See Ya Around" (http://www.cplrmh.com/). It will even guide your YA group in having their own newsletter.

It is best to provide the programs in a thematic series. Look for sponsors for the entire series, or underwriters for individual programs in the library. The better you are at getting good publicity, the easier it is to get sponsors. Having an art show or display area next to the programming area will allow you to do displays relevant to the program and opportunities to promote it. Your Chamber of Commerce might be a good source of not only funding programs relevant to business but can help with the publicity.

Programs for introducing people to the Internet and other technology tools have been very popular in many libraries. This is particularly good when you are seeking funding for new or improved technology. It provides an opportunity to show what a new system could do.

The Danville Public Library surveys its community to get their preferences for public library programming. You can check it out at http://www.dpl.lib.in.us/adultprogramsurvey.html. The University of Wisconsin School of Library and Information Science provides an online continuing education class for adult programming at http://www.slis.wisc.edu/continueed/adultPLprog.html.

Building Campaigns

The evolution of the library from the traditional, somewhat stuffy genre to the one where the library is a vibrant, community-based learning, and exploration center can be a powerful motivator for stakeholders. The Cerritos Public Library in California, described earlier, is one of the most successful public libraries in the world at transforming itself into an updated facility and program on a regular basis. They developed a pattern of regenerating their library every ten years. They replace or renovate the old building, add space and upgrade the infrastructure. They provide a case study in recombinant theory in action. One of their strengths has been the stability of the leadership team for the library. They cycled through two renewal programs with the same director, management team, and city leadership.

The opening of a new main library usually doubles or triples the average daily visitations by users, but it is important to take the systemic view of the entire library operation and not just a main library. Statistics show that the excitement and promotion of a new facility create a new group of stakeholders, increases the library's usage, and usually lead to increased funding. At the time of the design and construction of a new library it is possible to create a structure that can support a new vision and provide updated venues for programmatic changes. It is clear now that a successful library needs to provide the technology for online functions, self-service, and maximizing the use of the Internet. Now it is recognized, that communication spaces such as meeting rooms, perhaps small auditoriums, exhibit areas and showcases, and other spaces for group activities are necessary. Libraries have become much more social spaces than in the past.

The most successful main library campaigns have been connected with a program to renovate all of the branches and to build new ones in underserved areas. When neighborhoods are jealous of the main library they feel like isolated islands in a big city.

Recently many libraries have been successful because they recognize the importance of the systemic view. The San Jose Public Library has been very successful in developing the entire system of not only the main and the branches of the public library, but also, because it is a joint university/public library project, the new building, situated on University grounds, revitalized the academic library at San Jose State University. Seattle Public Library also revitalized the entire system with their system-wide development plan.

Often a building is given the name of a prominent person either in the history of the community or in development of the library. Andrew Carnegie certainly got a lot of buildings named after him. In Pittsburgh, the entire library was named after him and a neighboring town changed its name to Carnegie with the award of their new building.

Often major donors can be encouraged to provide big bucks for the naming opportunity. While it seems more the practice in academic libraries, a number of public libraries carry the name of a donor. This is quite acceptable as long as it is clear that the name on the building is not the name of the library system. While naming opportunities can provide monies, the process used in approval of the acceptance and the terms need to be clear and open with the community and the stakeholders. If you are not careful, the library may become subject to criticism by members of the community and the staff for accepting donations from corporations in return for naming opportunities.

The condition and the terms of the donation must be clear in the documents to the donors. It should be made clear that while the donor would have their name prominently displayed in the library and would receive publicity for their efforts, the donation in no way entitled anyone to more consideration for policies, procedures, services, or influence over the operations of the library than any body else.

It is quite clear that the creation of the Harold Washington Main Library in Chicago grew out of the community support for a fitting monument for their mayor who had recently died. The city of Chicago had tried for decades to get funding for a new library. They even relocated their library functions to a former warehouse/department store in the hopes of getting a new one. The historic Carnegie building in Chicago was turned into a cultural and historical center, and it appeared for a while that they might never get the new one. Today, not only has Chicago operated the new main library for nearly a decade, it has rejuvenated the entire citywide system. In 2007, the mayor announced a substantial budget increase to create a strong library presence in every neighborhood of Chicago.

Diversity

Often a library has stagnated in its development and seems to be locked into a pattern of service to the white middle- or upper-class people who used to dominate the local political scene. Even lifestyle changes in communities can leave the library on an island of indifference. A campaign to bring in community members who seem to be disfranchised due to perceptual or physical barriers such as freeways, race or beliefs, cultural disenfranchisement, or even lack of literacy has been used very successfully in communities such as San Francisco and Seattle.

The campaign for private funding should set a standard of including anyone who wished to support the library. A goal of asking for stretch gifts (which are more than they ever thought that they could give) can be successful. Many of the nonprofits and foundations may adopt the same goal. Providing testimonials by affinity groups or foundations to other potential donors can be very effective. If you have researched the donor you have an idea about how much they can and might give. Ask them to stretch and go beyond what they have done in the past. It is a good pitch if you can make that the norm in a major campaign and have stories about people who do so can be moving to people.

Libraries need a special relationship with users who are physically challenged and have special needs for the services of the library. The library should have a committee from the visually disadvantaged community, audio disadvantaged community, and others with special needs. A new building provides the opportunity to include technology and trained staff to meet their special needs such as audio navigation tools for the visually impaired. Transmitters are placed within and around the building features such as elevators, stairs, doors to different areas, and navigation corridors that communicate to the device that the person receives at the special needs center. This system can be linked to a street navigation system that leads to service providers. Some cities are now using similar technology for visually handicapped persons at busy intersections.

The diversity of needs by age groups should also be factored in. The library should know of the needs of the children, young adults, adults starting families, adults approaching retirement, and senior citizens should all be educated to see themselves as stakeholders and supporters. It requires a different communications style for the different groups. Sometimes there is value in bringing the groups together such as having young adults providing story hours or young people instructing the seniors in the use of the Internet.

Community Building

One of the strengths of a good library is its ability to create, or rejuvenate a sense of community among the residents. Ben Bagdikian a former dean of the School of Journalism at University of California–Berkeley was an early exponent of the need for local institutions to assume this role. He was the "canary in the mineshaft" in presenting the case that the massification of the media into a handful of corporations that span the globe, yet ignore the local community, has on local communities, discourse, and civility. He presented a very reasoned rational for the support, and even creation of local community communication channels in order to sustain the presence of community (http://www.thirdworldtraveler.com/Media/MediaMonopoly_Bagdikian.html).

Another seminal thinker and writer was John Gardner. He articulated the need for the survival of traditional community shared values in a world increasingly becoming focused on individualistic, hedonistic, and economic ascendancy goals. After a distinguished career of public service in government, his last official post was at the Hoover Institute at Stanford where he analyzed the lessons learned from all of his public service experience. The need for building community, and the ability for the library to contribute to the process appeals to many civic-minded people (http://www.pbs.org/johngardner/).

Meredith Farkas talks about the ability of the new technology to build new communities and to reconnect old ones. Her concepts, applied to public libraries, provide tremendous energy to the communities and individuals (Farkas, January 2007).

Go for Excellence

The concept of excellence in organizations and even libraries is not new and many people may get turned off by it being a cliché. While it does seem to be overused and thus trite, there is one really good use of the concept. It is a difficult sell to get people to donate to a government institution activity. The public libraries in this country have reached the stage where people expect them to be in their community and expect the government to pay for them. Attempts may be made to reduce the library budget because of the financial status of the community, or the pet programs of the decision makers, but in general the libraries are here to stay. Sometimes they are dangled by the governing body as being subject to not only reduction in funding but outright nonfunding. However, decision makers know fully well that the community will rally to come up with additional funds. On the other hand government programs are not characterized in the mind of the average taxpayer as providing excellence.

The perception is often that excellence costs money and that government functions tend toward mediocrity at best and downright ineptness and corruption at worst. However, the concept of your library having the goal of excellence in your programs or in your entire system can generate additional funds needed from nongovernmental sources. This goal can provide a good rational for the philanthropic community to participate. It makes a good platform from which to ask for their support.

Set targets along the way and assess progress regularly. If your strategy is working, keep going, if not, then find a new one. Try to keep the momentum up.

PRIVATE FUNDING CAMPAIGNS

An old saying by professional fundraisers is that people give money to people, not institutions. Sometimes people donate to a library without knowing any of the leadership or personnel in the library, but it is important that the people representing the library should be respected and trusted. This increases your ability to raise private money for the library. It is a basic principle of selling to cultivate a relationship of trust with a customer. This is even more important when cultivating donors.

Another strategy that is often used by foundations and other funders is to leverage their donations through a challenge or matching gift. You can find one person, foundation, or grant-making organization who will agree to put up one dollar for every dollar received from other donors up to a maximum amount. A time limit is usually set for you to raise the match. Both donors get their tax exemption and working together provides a larger donation. It is very important that your program locates the donors and researches the capability and interests of the donors.

Make sure you ask for the right amount of money. It is almost worse to ask for too little than to ask for too much. Most foundations make their requirements and interests available to potential donation seekers through their Web sites. Sometimes they are localized or focused in their area of interest. If you can meet their requirements, make a good case, show your ability to meet their stipulations, and have a good cause, your chance of success is high.

Scan your local area for small, local family, or corporate foundations. Try to get leads from other community organizations, scanning the newspapers for leads, and networking. Look for angels who have connections with the philanthropic community who will champion your cause. A key to the success for private fundraising by many public librarians has been the support of an angel who believed in the cause of their libraries.

CORPORATE OR BUSINESS APPROACHES

Corporations used to routinely provide grants or donations to good causes. Now they seem to be more driven by marketing enhancement for sales or services. Usually the corporation prefers to donate services, goods, or equipment that they manufacture. This can be used to your advantage if you know what service, good, or equipment you need and how it will match other services, goods, or equipment you are receiving elsewhere.

It is important to find out the geographic focus for corporate philanthropy. For example, large banks tend to see the library as a local cause and thus size their grants accordingly. They may take the approach that your campaign was really a local campaign and while they will donate, they will size their donations as local rather than regional or statewide. You will do better with the corporations that have leaders who are vested in the local community. An exception may be where corporations were started by local business people who retained their civic philanthropy even after the corporation had grown into major corporations.

MAJOR CAPITAL CAMPAIGNS

It is rare that a city, county, state, or even private entities fund the capital needs of the library through ongoing appropriations. Many librarians outside of the United States are envious of two rather unique features of capital projects in the United States. First is the ability of the governmental entity, with the approval of the voters, to issue bonds against future revenues for capital construction projects. It makes a lot of sense since, generally speaking, by the time enough money has been set aside, the cost of construction has escalated, and often the population is growing so that future residents get to pay for a facility that they may use for decades, and it is rare that elected officials will raise enough revenues in the regular taxing process to cover the costs.

The other American trait that surprises many foreign colleagues is that librarians can, and do raise private money. That is not a practice or tradition in many countries. Although this country has many private foundations that will not supplement any government-funded programs, there are many who do.

Family Foundations

Sometimes families establish foundations to honor parents, or other family members. Most of these are from families who have a strong philanthropic tradition. Other times it is a way to perpetuate support for their favorite causes or charities. It might even be for tax purposes, although the Internal Revenue Service (IRS) has cracked down on the tax exemptions of many foundations that are family controlled. Private family foundations are separate entities and are privately funded by the family. They are created with the specific purpose of contributing to various charitable causes, and it is a way to preserve their family name for many years to come. Private family foundations have certain legal requirements that they must meet. For example, they must distribute at least 5 percent of its assets each year. While they may have many other goals they must provide donations on a regular basis (Save Wealth Estates). A good example of good information about a major family foundation is available at the Paul Allen Foundation (http://www.pgafoundations.com/).

Another one is the Bill and Melinda Gates Foundation, which explains the interests of the foundation but they generally don't accept unsolicited proposals. They prefer to decide on the recipients based on their own information sources and goals of their foundation at the time (http://www.gatesfoundation.org/ForGrantSeekers/UnitedStates/).

Go to the Foundation Center Online Directory and start with those in your local and spread your search out to non-local foundations that have program goals that fit your need (http://foundationcenter.org/).

Library Foundations

While libraries are not classified as a charity as defined by the IRS, they are usually governmental entities for which donations are treated as tax deductible by the IRS. The FOL and library foundations should be set up as an entity to receive donations that are tax deductible for the donors. If the foundation gives property, the foundation avoids capital gains tax. Earnings on the foundation assets are tax-exempt.

Community Foundations

The San Francisco Foundation was the first community foundation in the country and has been successful in meeting the goals of the donors. The concept is that there are people who wish to contribute their money to charitable causes but do not want to select recipients nor manage the money can donate to the community foundation with some general parameters as to the causes that they support and the community foundation will invest the funds, manage the selection of the recipients, provide them with the funds based on their proposals, and report to the donors the outcomes of the projects. The money from many donors can be pooled together to make a grant that has more impact than otherwise possible.

Many community foundations are found throughout the United States. A local community foundation may not only provide grants, they might be willing to manage funds of a library foundation with all of the attendant fiscal responsibilities. If you can have this service it will give your foundation instant respectability in the eyes of major donors. The Natrona County Public Library works closely with several community foundations in Casper and Wyoming to achieve challenge funds as well as creditability to their campaign.

The Pike's Peak Library District (PPLD) received a grant for $240,000 to expand services to seniors in 2007. These funds came from the Colorado Trust's Healthy Aging Initiative (PPLD grant, 2007). More and more trusts or foundations are becoming very narrowly focused. It is important that the library keeps up with the new foundations and trusts that are taking place.

The Los Angeles Public Library lists around sixty recent gifts, many of which are from local foundations. A number of Hollywood celebrities have foundations that have donated to the library (http://www.lfla.org/foundation/accomplishments.php). Leonardo DeCaprio Charitable Foundation was one. The library has had a long time historic association with Gregory Peck.

While your community may not have a media celebrity, you may have others who can champion the library. Looking at the way other foundations work can help you enlist their support in the creation of a library foundation.

AFFINITY GROUPS

The involvement of affinity groups may be the most ground-breaking element for your campaign. They can be organized around any central shared interest group ranging from cultural heritage groups to social issues groups. It appears that the concept has become a popular strategy for creating stakeholder groups who give back to the library. It appears that it is pretty popular since a Google search on "library affinity groups" turns up 1,750,000 hits that include Loyola University, Wagner College, the Anarchist Library, the Neuroscience History Archives, and Juniata College among others.

A policy for the formation, procedures, and expectations for each affinity group should be adopted and they should be applied equitably to all who express interest. While it is good to give them recognition for their efforts, it should be also understood that the management of the resources and the programs rests with the library. This strategy creates the ability to reach out to individuals who have never felt vested in the library.

GOVERNMENT SOURCES

It is important to get seed money for your development program. Use starter money to hire someone to write the proposals. There is also good information at the ALA Web site at http://www.libraryhq.com/funding.html and at http://infotoday.com/searcher/nov03/becker.shtml and http://www.npguides.org.

Major dollars are available in one-time grants that in some cases may extend for up to three years. For the immediate future, Institute for Museum and Library Services is a good place to look for national funding.

ONLINE FUNDING

The Institute for Politics has an interesting article on political fundraising online that point out an area for further exploration. They include a piece titled Democracy and the Internet in collaboration with the Campaign Finance Institute which points out that online giving has increased dramatically in the past election campaigns. The political parties and candidates have really ramped up their efforts of the Internet not only to communicate with supporters and voters but also to make it easy for them to contribute to the campaigns. While the article doesn't really tell you how to do it, it points out that people online are more likely to be politically active, almost half of small online donors contacted the campaign first, that in the 2004 presidential election more than 80 percent of those who were 18 to 34 of age donated online. They go on to state, "Online fundraising will be central to the future of campaign fundraising" (Institute for Politics). It does lead one to consider the potential for online solicitation and giving through the Internet. You do have to be careful to not appear to supporting public voting issues with taxpayer's money. It was surprising to find that the Westerville Ohio Public Library advocated for the passage of a renewal of a tax levy right on their home page. The information presented seems evenhanded and factual but could raise eyebrows of people who are concerned about tax funding to support a particular side in an election. Critics of the library in many cities would create uproar if their librarian advocated a political issue on its Web site. On the other hand the use of third party organizations such as the FOL or a library foundation makes a lot of sense.

It would be easy to put a button on your library's home page for how you can help the library, which could lead to the Friends, the Foundation, and the volunteer program. It can also be used to recruit users for allied groups such as the adult literacy program. People will help the library in many ways, but in fundraising circles it is an old adage that you won't get money unless you ask for it. The Web site and other technology tools provide an opportunity to broadcast the case statement of the library and then to allow the reader to become energized through online communications. Thus, a person looking for library resources such as books, online journals, or other services on the Web site can be educated in the value of the institution and how they can help to achieve the vision of the library.

The Metropolitan Group presented some interesting data about online giving at the ALA annual conference in 2006. They contend that at that time 73 percent of Americans use the Internet, 42 percent have broadband connection, and most importantly there is a strong correlation among people who are connected and those who have resources for giving. Online giving has grown from around .55 billion dollars in 2001 to around 4.53 billion dollars in 2005. This is quite a jump and is probably going to increase even faster. Research shows that online donors give more. Their average gift is $57 as compared to $33 for traditional giving and the revenue per donor is $114 compared to $82. The interactive nature of online communications is a big plus for giving. You get good feedback on your contacts.

LOCAL REFERENDUMS

Often times you must take action by going to the voters to protect the services and resources that you already have or need for the future. These may include referendums to increase taxes, to overcoming state limits on local spending, to provide temporary tax limit overrides, to allocating a certain amount of the city's budget, and to establishing a library specific government authority. In general they all require the library to go to the voters.

The campaigns are similar regardless of the issue. Usually there are only two ways to get to the voters: have the elected officials put it on the ballot, or get a certain number of voter signatures to force a referendum. The tax limitations that were imposed by Proposition 13 in California put severe limitations on the ability of local jurisdictions to either allow the tax revenues to rise in tune with the inflationary increases in property values or to increase taxes to deal with new or existing infrastructure and operational needs. Libraries have been particularly affected by these meat axe approaches to keeping taxation low, or actually reducing it significantly such as in Oregon.

When this happens, it provides a stimulus to many local jurisdictions to go to the voters to get special tax funds for libraries in order to provide room for other programs such as fire, police, and general administration outside their regular budget cap. This strategy allows the elected officials to take credit if the election succeeds and to say the voters didn't want it if it fails. It is a win-win situation for the elected official. If this has happened to you, you might try this strategy, too.

For most librarians it means that not only do they have to think outside the historic box of the traditional local government cycle by getting the money to include private donations, grants, and ongoing fundraising in their budgets, they have to be prepared to keep their ability to get traditional government funding as well. Many times the only relief from the statewide referendums on tax caps or expenditure level rollbacks means that you must be prepared to go to the voters in their localities every few years. You must be prepared for having a regular cycle of local elections to just keep your budget, let alone to get more.

Tax Limitation Overrides

In California as in other locations, some county librarians must go to the voters regularly in order to get their budgets increased beyond the cap established by the state propositions. The fact that the community has grown in population and other factors are irrelevant since the cap is based on a fixed percentage of the previous amount of revenues. This makes it difficult to deal with issues such as increased salaries for the employees, staffing new facilities, and having the funds to deal with the changing expectations and wants of the stakeholders. These overrides are for a defined period of time and in many states it takes a 2/3rds approval to pass. If you are in such a situation it is imperative that you incorporate the steps needed into your strategic development plan and consider it an ongoing function and not just something that happens once in a while.

It will be critical for you to have a program for stakeholder creation and ongoing development. You will have to pay attention to issues such as customer service, pride in the library by the community, and constant evaluation of the management and operations.

Increasing Statutory Limitations

When the revenue for the library is obtained from a tax specific to a regional library district, it is often capped by the state. The statute that allowed the creation and operation of regional library districts in Colorado required that a regional library district must receive majority approval by the voters in two or more legal jurisdictions. The statute also capped the mill levy for regional library districts at $1\frac{1}{2}$ mill and had been at that level for some time.

If, as in Colorado, you are faced with a period of rapid population growth that requires significant investment in infrastructure or the library budget has not kept up with the needs of the stakeholders, the only way to get the budget up is to go to the voters. But before that the state statutory limitation has to be raised. It is a lot easier to get the local community to vote the authority for an increase than to get the state legislature to approve it. Since Colorado had mostly city and county libraries that would not be affected by this law, it was pretty much up to the regional library districts.

This is the time when active and supportive FOL and other support groups can really make a difference. The first challenge is getting the bill introduced. The next challenge is the committee process and then the house, senate, and governor's approval. The final step is to take it to the voters and get it approved. This process may take over two years, and it certainly requires a lot of hard work. The whole process may need to be repeated several years later.

These strategies not only require an active Community Resource Office (CRO) but it also means that the director and other leaders in the library support groups be very active in social, cultural, and civic activities. Participation in the Chamber of Commerce and meetings by the city, county, and the state are important. Issues or problems often face a local government that you can assist in solving. If you take the approach that the library can and should provide professional advice and management to local governments or communities on information access issues, you can demonstrate the library's value to the local government officials in solving some of their problems.

Bond Issues

One of the most important tools for obtaining major funding for library capital improvements is the bond issue. The local authority usually has statutory authority to issue bonds to be repaid from future revenues if the voters approve the proposition in an election. This strategy is often used because the funds come from future revenue which includes revenue from new residents when the community is growing. It allows having all the money available up front prior to construction of a new library, if that is your project. This is nearly impossible if the money comes from annual appropriations.

This process is somewhat unique to the United States and has been a major factor in the development of new library facilities in the country since the 1960s. If you have good relationship with your local elected officials, it is not too difficult to convince them to put the issue before the voters. If it passes, the elected officials can take credit for its success, and if it fails, they can attribute the responsibility for the defeat to the voters. It is usually, a win-win situation for them. Since it goes to the voters, it will also override the limitations in tax caps or expenditure limits. In general the voters have the final say in these issues.

Sometimes, as it happened in California, the state legislature and governor have supported statewide bond issues for library construction. Billions of dollars have been obtained from this strategy. The state library solicits, assists the local libraries in the preparation of their applications, then coordinates a committee of state elected and appointed officials to award the grants.

In some cases, when there was no authority for a library or a regional library district to have bond issues for new construction, it will be necessary to go to the legislature to get authority for the local voters to make the decision. A very important step may when you are able to convince the local school district that land that they had declared surplus should be donated to the library for a new library or a new regional library. These processes vary from state to state and need to be researched, but companies such as those that handle the financial arrangement for selling and managing the bonds will have a vested interest in the financial success of the project. They should provide voluntary consultative service.

You will need to check your state's statutes to see if they prohibit the expenditure of bond funds for furniture and equipment. In some states this is not only accepted but also encouraged. It might even be possible to use bond funds for additional books or other resources for your collection.

This somewhat minor provision in the laws of the different states will have a major impact on your project. It may not be necessary for the library to raise significant outside funds for the furniture and equipment of the library, although your FOL group may want to help with a first-class dedication for the local community. If you cannot use bond money for furniture, equipment, or even building enhancements, you will need to raise money since it is not likely that these will come from the regular city budget.

Revenue Entitlements

Perhaps one of the best strategies for strategic funding is the creation of an entitlement for the library requiring the local government to budget a set proportion of its budget to the library. You will find little in the literature about this relating to libraries, although it has happened for education in many states. A Google search on education revenue entitlements pulls up over 700,000 hits, many of which are coming from state or federal mandates. The only relevance of this information is to research for ones that include money for libraries in some way or schools that have developed good strategies for getting the entitlement established or funded. A Google search for public library entitlements will pull up some hits, but the only area when funding entitlements seems to be under consideration is in the United Kingdom. Based on a presentation at the International Federation of Library Associations (IFLA) Congress in 2007, the strategy has not been very successful in ensuring funding for public libraries there.

Another way to get an entitlement is to get specific language in federal or state legislation that makes funding a requirement. This takes a great deal of time and effort on your part and requires a long-term strategy. A good time for you to attempt it is as a follow-up to a successful building campaign. The stakeholders can understand the need for increased funding if they are getting a new building which will have many more users and services.

A few years ago the library supporters in Wisconsin tried to get a state law amended to require local authorities to provide 13 percent of their local budget to their public library. Their research showed that on average it was only 9 percent. The campaign is still part of the lobbying effort by the Wisconsin Library Association. Wisconsin is also one of several states that have legislation requiring maintenance of effort for local library budgets in order for the public library to belong to a state-funded network. This strategy is relatively easy to sell if you emphasize that the reason this is needed is so that the local library doesn't use the state funding for their networks as a reason to lower their own budgets and thus shift the funding of the local library to the state. Wisconsin law requires municipalities to fund libraries at a level not lower than the average of the previous three years to retain membership in a public library system and remain eligible for state funding. South Carolina, Utah, and California are other examples of mandated maintenance of effort.

At the national level, ALA is pushing to get school librarians, or library media specialists, added to the category used for teachers in the "No Child Left Behind" act so that their salaries can come from federal funds. Without that, school librarians are extremely vulnerable to budget cutting from the districts having to refocus local funds to accomplish goals in the act.

Other countries have entitlements. Entitlements for schools in Australia seem to be quite established and in the United Kingdom there is discussion on library entitlements;

but it generally refers to the entitlement of communities and individuals to have library service. Standards have been set as goals but never anything as drastic as an entitlement by the local government. Although there is a very thorough presentation of public library standards in Wales, it doesn't directly address the funding other than an annual budget expense by the Welsh National Government that is provided as a subsidy to local authorities. They seem to have a comprehensive set of goals and a process for monitoring the local libraries (http://new.wales.gov.uk/topics/cultureandsport/museumsarchiveslibraries/cymalL4/libraries_local/WPLS/WPLS02-051/?lang=en).

The Fort Vancouver Library District was established in 1950 and is the oldest library district in Washington (http://www.fvrl.org/aboutus/index.cfm). In the 1960s, the local governments and state government in Colorado joined to provide a mechanism to allow small libraries to join into regional library districts to become more efficient and effective libraries. It would provide smaller libraries with fewer resources to join with a major city to form a regional library district. Local jurisdictions who wanted to participate placed the issue on their ballot. If their voters approved, the district would be established. If voters in one of the original jurisdictions failed to approve the question on the ballot, they would not be in the district. Other jurisdictions could go ahead and form their own. This resulted in the establishment of the regional library districts.

A good example of a success in a relatively new library district is the Rampart Library District in Colorado. They passed two bonds, one of which provided funding for new libraries in the district and one to pay for additional staff and materials. *American Libraries* provides an annual update on public library expenditures that reference some of the more successful library initiatives. *American Libraries* online provides a summary of referendums on a regular basis (http://www.ala.org/ala/alonline/selectedarticles/1206_ReferendaRoundup.pdf).

In 2006 there were successful referendums in Washington at the Vancouver Public Library, in Oregon at the Multnomah County Library, in California at the Los Angeles Public Library, and Utah at the Brigham City Library. Texas, New York, Pennsylvania, North Carolina, and Louisiana all had successful public referendums.

The argument that the joining two or more public libraries in order to provide better service and efficiency can be quite compelling. Once you have an independent taxing authority, you reduce the dialog about funding issues to between the library and the citizens. While you may need local, regional, or state support to get it started, after that your destiny is much more in your hands.

RUNNING CAMPAIGNS FOR REFERENDUMS

Getting Started

At this point it is assumed that all of the homework in Chapters 2, 3, 4 has been completed or at least most of the elements are operative. One of the challenges is what tasks need to be done first. You can be very rational and layout the steps with timelines with formal systems such as used by engineers or computer scientists. Often the basic diagram is the flow charts with tasks, directions, merge points, and results. This is a very rational approach. It is important to use this as a tool to keep on track and to educate participants in the process. An example of a step-by-step process is given in Appendix A.

It also needs to be understood that much of politics is not precise and planned. Part of the strategy has to be like a picture puzzle. Sometimes you have ten pieces that come together in a rational fashion like the image of a big red barn. You can click in those pieces quickly. Then there are those pieces over which you have little control. It is the same with decision making. It is often thought best to make quick decisions, but it is important that you have adequate information, knowledge, and personnel to make the decision. Sometimes you have to put part of the puzzle or process aside until you have more information, build more support, or have the funds to proceed. This does not lessen the importance of taking the tasks and organize and prioritize them on a regular basis. You may want to create a new list weekly with a formal process involving others quarterly.

Researching and Obtaining Legal Support and Authority

Before beginning any campaign for funding, you will need to check the legal authority for your plans. This is especially important in planning to remodel, add on to, or build a new facility. If you are adding to or remodeling a building that has been designated a historical landmark, the planning and approval process can be very complicated and take years to get all of the approvals. You may need a number of studies to get the go ahead with a building project.

In San Francisco, we were required to do four studies concerning the placement of the library and other studies to determine the funding potential. First was a study to assess the potential for the existing library to expand on its current site. The second was a complete engineering and seismic analysis of the existing main library. The third one was an analysis of the maximum building area available within existing zoning requirements on the site, and the fourth was an alternative-use evaluation study of the existing library. As a result the decision was made to build a new main library, that it had to fit the architectural style and dimensions of civic center, and that the old library would move to the Asian Art Museum which would renovate the old building and move out of their Golden Gate Park site that they shared with the Museum of Fine Arts (Dowlin and Smulyan, 1993, p. 49).

An independent study was conducted to determine the ability to raise money for furniture, equipment, and building enhancements was conducted by a national fundraising firm. The study was critical for three reasons:

1. A large number of competing fundraising campaigns were underway by major cultural institutions.
2. The city's philanthropic community has a limited size.
3. The institute had received most all of their monies from the government and had little history of raising large amounts of money (Dowlin and Smulyan, 1993, p. 52).

These studies not only provided information for decision making, an added value came since they were presented in public venues—they helped educate the community and its leaders in the value of the project.

The legal authority for your building project may be already granted to the local government, and it may not be necessary to get any new legislation passed. This must be checked if your library is an Independent Taxing Authority because you may have to get the legal authority for a vote and issuance of the bonds for a capital project.

Your project may be a part of a larger bond issue by the city or county and if so close coordination needs to take place by all involved in the campaign. The success of library issues sometimes leads the elected officials to put the library project into a citywide infrastructure issue. While it could seem a good strategy for the city, it could prove to be a liability for your library; however, library issues tend to pass much more often than infrastructure issues in the local government.

You must locate any legal restraints upon public employees and campaign participants and provide the information to everyone involved in the campaign. Federal, state, and local statutes may limit your library employees from campaigning on work time. It is a fine line between free speech of a person and using library resources for campaigning, and guidelines are needed for all your employees whether they participate in the campaign or not. Also IRS regulations place limitations on the amount of funds and determination of which activities are allowed for tax-exempt organizations. These legal rules change all of the time. They not only need to be complied with for legal reasons but irregularities in financing or campaigning which tend to generate negative publicity and can be used by the opponents. You may want to involve consultants that specialize in assessing the feasibility of a project early as part of your research phase.

Creating the Case Statement

It is clear that, if you are going to raise money, you need to create a case statement that will be the anchor for the communications for the effort. It is rare that funders will actually read, digest, and internalize a strategic plan. In the case statement you take the elements that are core and create a convincing argument as to why the project should be done. A good start for nonprofits and libraries is presented by the Minnesota Council of Nonprofits (Minnesota Council). They recommend that the statement be limited to one page. It is often a 1–4 page presentation (Web, print, blog, or whatever) that is used to support the selling of the program. Nice pictures of people, testimonials by users, and donors help make the campaign real.

A case statement from Lehigh University has a lot of good phrases such as "Linderman Library Transformed," "More than Books and Beauty," "A Dynamic Intellectual Center," "A Strong Tradition," "A Strong Foundation," and "Linderman Unbound." It makes a good linkage from the past to the present to the future (http://www.lehigh.edu/lts/linderman/case.pdf). Even small public libraries find value in a good case statement. An example is Alamogordo Public Library in New Mexico (http://aplfound.org/pages/casestatement.html).

A fairly recent strategy is to calculate how much the library costs per service and then calculate the benefit to the community. Cost per benefit analysis has been around for a long time but using it for libraries is relatively new. Former Director of the St. Louis Public Library Glen Holt has refined the process and the message in a way that is easily replicated (Holt). The objectives of the Public Benefits Valuation Study are quite detailed and specific. They include:

1. To construct as an analytical framework a matrix that identifies categories of patrons and service use common to the five major (but distinct) urban public libraries participating in the study;
2. To identify the nature of benefits received by each class of patron for each type of service used;
3. To develop survey and database methods of measuring the direct benefits of library services to each of the classes of patrons;
4. To quantify these benefits in current dollars to permit calculation of the return to annual taxpayer investment in each of the five participating libraries;

5. To develop effective means of communicating to library constituents and to the general public the meaning of the estimated return and the value derived from taxpayer investment in their library;
6. To evaluate the success of the framework, survey instruments, benefit measures, and communication strategies with respect to:
   a. The value of the analytical framework in assisting a library's administrators to visualize their mission in terms of the service menu provided to specific submarkets within their customer base;
   b. The value of the analytical framework in assisting library administrators to quantify the impacts of effective allocation and delivery of services on perceived direct benefits by classes of customers;
   c. The extent to which the framework provides a defensible floor for the estimated return to public investment in urban libraries, individually and for the five libraries as representative urban libraries;
   d. The extent to which information about the return to taxpayer investment influences constituent and taxpayer attitudes toward urban libraries;
   e. The degree to which the methodology developed is cost effective and transportable to other urban libraries.
7. To disseminate the results of the study and train administrators of other major urban libraries in applying the transportable methodology to calculate their own estimates of return to taxpayer investment (Holt).

The blog by Farkas on Demonstrating Impact, Value, and ROI at http://www.libsuccess.org/index.php?title=Demonstrating_Impact%2C_Value_and_ROI provides a current and ongoing discussion on the topic.

The Metropolitan Group is very active in assisting libraries to get the money through different strategies. They define a case statement as telling the story to potential donors. They include "the stories of why an organization, program or service is necessary to its community and how it will impact lives" (Metropolitan Group Case Statement). It is important that you use different stories with the different stakeholders so that you can maximize the impact. The Kanawha County Public Library in West Virginia has an excellent case statement on their Web site. It also translates into an attractive brochure (Kanawha County Public Library). Another attractive case statement is from Yale University and can be viewed at http://yaletomorrow.yale.edu/pdfs/libe28spt06.pdf.

Expanding the Go-to-Team

Once the decision is made to undertake the development program the members of the Go-to-Team will have to be expanded. As you get more and more specialties and people involved, it is also important to keep your primary Go-to-Team small. They should serve as liaisons of the other teams and regularly discuss what is happening with the primary team as well as communicate to the other teams regularly.

If you have not had an excellent and supportive lawyer or a financial expert on your team, it is time to get them. Both of them should have experience in their fields dealing with political campaigns and if they provide leadership to a segment of the community such as the local bar association, that is a plus. Your FOL should be the first place to look. It is also best to get the attorney(s) for the city or county on your side as well. They may not need to be a regular at meetings but they should be knowledgeable and supportive of the project. If your campaign involves a referendum, it will be necessary to involve many more people because of the process of getting the signatures to place the issue on the ballot.

Some members who are politicians have to be brought in. Experts are needed for various tasks such as a preliminary design and costing plan by architects. It will be important for you to bring in professionals in fundraising, political campaigns, community building, and a variety of other players. These people all have to be educated to your vision and strategic goal, and this takes time. It is critical that, if they do not buy in to the project, they need to be replaced by people who are not only committed but passionate about the project.

Team building is important here. You may need to involve team-building professionals. If you are the director, it may not work for you to try to be the team builder and the director. You also need to have a regular series of team-building events. This part is not as simple as it seems. It will take money to hire a professional for this part. You will need to have a venue that is conducive to the task, supporting materials, and communication. It is critical that your team members be supportive of the vision, mission, and goals of the library and committed to success.

Creating a Separate Campaign Committee

This is the time to formalize your expanded Go-to-Team into a campaign committee, as is usually required by law. This provides the authority to collect campaign funds and to expend them for the campaign. Your Go-to-Team should have someone knowledgeable in all the legalities of running a campaign. You should consider hiring a political consultant to assist in the development of the overall strategy at this point. You need enough starting funds to hire a campaign fundraiser, and, in a large city, a neighborhood outreach worker to ensure that all neighborhoods are brought into the mission, vision, and goals. Sometimes you may be able to get a prominent elected official such as the mayor to make a significant kick-off contribution that gets the fundraising rolling. Elected officials who have what is considered safe offices for reelection may be willing to contribute from their own campaign fund.

Polls

Information from valid and timely polls of the community can provide valuable clues to the attitudes of the public and the voters. A benchmark political survey at the start of the program provides the baseline of data for determining the probability of success and the messages that need to be given to the voters. You should be able to get a state or federal grant to do the planning that includes the polling process. The initial results can generally provide data on the perceptions of the individuals in the community. This data can provide a strong case for swaying the elected officials as well as helping you to design your strategy.

Perhaps the first poll should be a benchmark survey of the attitudes and perceptions of your library and its services as a whole. If your goal is a major funding campaign, then a second poll could be focused on the specific issue. Your community needs to believe

1. A new library is important for the education of the city's children,
2. The new library should be "world-class,"
3. A new library building is an important investment in the future.

This poll will indicate that if the issue was voted on at the time of the poll, it would receive a specific percentage of the vote. You can then decide if it is sufficient to pass or if it would be sufficient to pass but not enough for everyone to be comfortable, or it would not pass at all.

Another poll could be conducted in conjunction with a newspaper. This would predict what percentage of the vote would be in favor of the bond issue. During your campaign you should continue collecting information via polling to guide our campaign. A pollster might not only give the library a break on the cost of the polling, they might allow you to include specific questions on the library in polls for other political clients and issues. This allows you to shift your message based on feedback from the community throughout the campaign.

In a bond issue campaign, some people provide way too much information. Often you see the Christmas tree approach where a campaign tries to put something in for everybody. It can be too complicated for some people. Sometimes simpler is better.

Other sources of information may be available in your city. For example, another city office may conduct an annual survey of the people of the city in order to assess the attitude of the residents toward the city, its services, and its departments. When this survey shows that one of the most respected departments in the city is the public library, you will be comfortable to start your project.

Consultants

Experts need to be added to the team who are knowledgeable about precinct-level research and communications, organization of the political tactics, and communication to the voters. A member of your Go-to-Team who is politically connected may be working with an effective campaign consultant and this may help in funding the cost for that consultant. Please remember that your library must appear to be neutral in its politics. If you do not have someone in mind, it is probably advisable for you to issue a request for proposal (RFP) from several consultants. Your goal for selection should be based on the consultant's track record of success, knowledge of how to be effective in your local community, and a good organizational fit.

Currently, consultant firms are becoming specialized in library fundraising and election campaigns. You can contact directors of libraries who have been successful and check out ALA's online directory of consultants at the ALA Web site. Another source is an independent consultant's directory, which includes firms that list expertise in fundraising at http://www.libraryconsultants.org/research.asp. You will also need to include consultants for the local politics and specialized tasks such as acquiring signatures on the referendum petitions and operating phone banks toward the end of the campaign.

Endorsements

Having written, oral, or media testimony by prominent people, politicians, and avid supporters in the official ballot handbook is important in any community. A solid and enthusiastic lineup of endorsements is critical for success in any election issue. Your endorsements should include neighborhood activists, business organizations, politicians, prominent socialites, and just plain people. It is important to seek out spokespersons for diverse groups such as gay and lesbian, African Americans, Latino, and other groups.

In many communities the League of Women Voters will put out informative pamphlets for the community before elections. You need to be sure to get your information in their handbook and in all probability they will endorse the library's proposal. You can find your local affiliate at http://www.lwv.org/AM/Template.cfm?Section=Find_a_Local_League.

Some entrepreneurs or political support groups will put your issue on their handouts, doorknob hangers, and posters. Usually you have to pay for this service. The concept of slate cards seems to be quite prominent in large cities. If you have never heard of them you might want to check out http://www.granick.com/blog/?p=498.

You need to be careful about who you partner with when you are considering using the collaborative approach. You might find yourselves in collaboration with an extreme group that turns voters off. Talk with your local politicians or consultants about what is most effective in your community.

GAINING MOMENTUM

You have done all the preliminary steps of polling the citizens to assess their level of support, raising money for planning, doing the planning, and getting legal approval to the issue on the ballot. You are off and running and there is no going back. At this point you need to shift the focus of the effort on the most likely voters. They need to be educated and motivated to support the library. Here is where your political consultants come in. They should have already done the research on the voting patterns in the local election. One good clue for predicting library support will be past voting records on school bond or financing issues. Another one is to look for precincts that have a good track record of voting for civic projects. Look for precincts where there is a large voter turnout and look at their voting patterns. While you can get this information from your local city clerk, you probably need the consultant to interpret the data for you.

With this information different tactics can be employed in three different segments of the voters. The first one is to send a nice note to those who almost always support education and civic projects thanking them for their past support and encouraging them to not only support your issue but to convince their neighbors to do likewise. The second tactic is for precincts that always vote against education or civic projects. You just send a note hoping that they will support the issue and provide them with brief information about what it will mean to them and their community when it is successful. The third tactic, which is the most important, is to target those precincts that have swing voters. Target them specifically to ensure that they not only vote for your issue but that they get actively involved in support.

Getting the Money for the Campaign

At this point you need to establish a budget for the campaign. If you have a local consultant, they should have a good idea of the various costs. It could vary significantly from community to community. Your local politicians who you have cultivated, or converted, will help on that as well. A look at the breakdown of sources of funding would include the FOL. Large ticket events or smaller receptions can be helpful. Supporters in general and members of the fundraising team can obtain funds from small and large businesses. Most elected officials will contribute some amount to the campaign. This is pretty standard practice for elected officials who have surpluses in their campaign funds. You should make a list similar to the one below:

- Friends of the Library
  Three levels of solicitation are used for your FOL. This group contributes from their treasury, they can have events to raise money, or they can contribute as individuals. They can be reached through the normal communication channels of your FOL. Their newsletters, emails, and meetings provide opportunities. Since they already see themselves as stakeholders in your library, they should provide a good start to the campaign fund. It is good to provide recognition for their efforts as soon as possible. The members of your FOL are the best place to start to recruit volunteer workers for the election. Ask the people who organize the book sale to help organize part of the campaign program. Ask all of them to help with the speaker's bureau, door to door campaigning, and telephone banks.

- Elected Officials
  Send a letter to every elected official in the community explaining how important the library's project is to them personally, their family their neighborhood, and their city. If they are school district officials, stress the library's future ability to help educate the children.

- Prominent Citizens

  Most civic leaders feel responsible for the success of their community and can be very helpful with the business support for the campaign. Target one leader in the financial sector, one in the retail trade, and so on. Educate them to deliver the message around their community and organizations.

- Other Cultural Institutions

  Museums, the symphony, the community band, and other community cultural and literary institutions are all good candidates for support. If you can convince the president of their board or their director to sell the project their stakeholders, you multiply your own ability to communicate.

Today, an online solicitation and contribution program can be very successful. You can establish a solid ongoing relationship with stakeholders and provide them with as much information as they want. They can easily donate by credit card and may even get a trip to Hawaii through the large amount placed on their credit card.

Speakers' Bureau

Expand and focus the speakers' bureau that you set up back in the start of the book. Train them in the issues for the campaign and provide them with printed material and a campaign committee contact to answer questions for which they weren't prepared. Be sure to follow up on new questions that arise by providing the answer to that speaker and in sharing it with all of the speakers.

Door-to-Door Campaigning

Some of the most effective sales pitches can happen in your door to door campaigns. Volunteers canvass the neighborhoods. If someone is home give them a brief sales pitch. If no one answers the door put campaign hangers on the doorknob. Be sure to orient and train the volunteers to provide information for follow-up or more questions. A Web site of the campaign organizers is perfect for this kind of orientation. It could keep the workers up to the minute as well as keep their enthusiasm up. It is best if the neighborhoods are targeted so that the energy goes to the right place.

Telephone Banks

The members of your FOL, the Foundation, library staff, the library administration, and other volunteers will spend hours on the telephone during the weeks leading up to the election. To reduce the chance of angering your recipients, make sure you don't call during dinner hours or other inconvenient times. If you have funding to do so, you may wish to hire a specialist who will set up the phone bank, train the volunteers, and track the success of the calls. Look for a business like a major bank to donate their office phones in the evening when they aren't using them. You must organize the volunteers, and use the central switchboard to place the calls. When someone says, "hello," your volunteer swings into action. It is surprising to find that most people say that they support the library and plan to vote for the issue. In that case you should urge them to talk to their neighbors and friends as well. Be prepared for the people that seem to enjoy the conversation and will tell you their favorite anecdote about the library. The volunteers must be prepared to get off the line politely and go to the next call.

Opposition

Many people may be opposed to the library issue for a variety of reasons. They may not want to change the present library or they may insist that the old library should be renovated rather than building a new one. They may not be swayed by the studies that show that a renovation would cost as much as a new one, would shut down the main library for years, and would only gain a limited amount of additional space. They need to learn that structures in the area where the present library is located may be legally limited by the planning and zoning code to a certain height, length, and width. The constraints of the old architecture make the cost of upgrading the infrastructure for the twenty-first-century library very large. Some other people don't want to spend the money on the main library; they want the money for the branches. These people can be easier to convince if they see that the goal is not just the one building but the entire library system. Your strategic plan and case statement should include all library facilities and services at the start. Then it can be prioritized as to when the phases will take place.

The number of people in the opposition to your project may never be very large but they may be very determined. They can take up a lot of time in public meetings making their points repeatedly. They may include a prominent state senator, an ex-city librarian, and some disgruntled library employees. They can be very adept at making sure that, if a campaign speaker appears on a talk show or other public venue, they appear as well. You should realize that your appearances are giving them opportunities that they never would have been able to get on their own. You should be selective in your venues. A group might organize informally to try to ensure that they are at as many of your opportunities possible and can be very determined in their efforts. If this situation occurs, you need to have done your homework and have the studies and polls to show that the library program is a good plan and that the people of the community will support it.

In the Home Stretch

This is the time to keep getting feedback and adjusting your message if necessary. Keep the momentum going and keep looking for clever ways to increase support. One clever idea is to provide transportation to the polls for people who need a ride. Ask your supporters for volunteers who can take people to the polls. While this may not be needed by very many people, the fact that you can offer it in your information gives a sense that the library and its supporters are caring people. You might buy transportation passes or try to get them donated and give them out to the needy. You do have to be careful that your campaign isn't accused of buying votes.

Down to the Wire

React to other political campaigns and information from your consultant and pollsters. Keep the Go-to-Team together and enthusiastic. Keep feeding them information and looking for areas that need emphasis. Keep motivating your supporters with events that bring them together so you can provide a pep talk and encourage each other.

Closing Out

Regardless of whether you have a victory or a defeat, you need to keep the group together, the mechanism in place, and the vision in mind. This gives you the opportunity, should you have lost, to fight another day. If you won, you will probably have another campaign in the library's future, and you can build on what you did in the first one. Some librarians have had to go through more than one defeat before they feel victory. Thank all of your stakeholders when you do succeed on posters, billboards, and written thank you notes. They will remember your thanks and be even more supportive the next time. Put signs on school buildings and libraries thanking voters for their support. They will remember your thanks and be even more supportive the next time. The major contributors and volunteers should receive something tangible like a plaque that includes a brick that was in the old library.

Regardless of the outcome keep everybody involved. Develop a new vision and keep on going. There are thousands of people who have a personal stake in the success of the library and the ones who give their money and their time need to be particularly recognized and feel valued.

7

The Keys to the Financial Castle Kitchen

It is time to bring all of these parts and fragments into closure with a strategy that you can use to be successful. It is important that the library leadership and the community realize that development must be a continuous cycle that evolves from visioning, to strategic planning, to evaluation, and then to implementation of organizational or technological changes. The library or library system will go through periods of tremendous change such as building a new main library, a major renovation, or implementing a new technology platform, all large ticket items. Then it will, perhaps, be quieter for a while but you must continue to respond to changes around it.

STRATEGIC THINKING AND FOCUS

The bottom line to a strategic development plan is change. You are either getting the resources to change to keep up with the community and societal changes or you want to change the library to lead the community in change. Even if a librarian does not want to change the library, there are many external changes that will continue to put pressure on them for change. Libraries will need more money because the public continues to expect newer and better service and resources even though there is constant competition from other public services for funding. The public still wants all the services that they have had in their library as well as the new ones. It is very clear that the computer and the Internet have changed the landscape of library operation and services, and it is difficult to predict what library services will be like in twenty years or beyond. There are major shifts in the way that libraries must operate that will require constant development and implementation funds in addition to operational dollars.

Raising local tax money isn't the only response to the challenges contained in these transitions. In considering the sources of funding it is important to locate and assess all possible funding sources and to consider other ways to either raise funds or reallocate existing funds. Examples include institutional efficiency increases, grants from private or other government sources, changing priorities to free up funds, shifting part of the print materials budget to online media, sharing costs with other libraries and organizations, sharpening existing functions, improved contract administration, fee-based revenues (per use or licensed), promotional offers, fees from the user or fees from the agency or department in the city or charges to a corporation, and possibly others.

One of the advantages of obtaining new funds is that you don't have to reduce existing programs and services. It increases your overall funding base and provides some security in developing numerous sources as opposed to one or two that might be modified drastically by some political happening. It does require investment. A well-run development program is required. Fund sources must be identified, researched, and proposals must be written and presented. This takes institutional resources. Often the external grants are for a short term only and often require matching funds or maintenance of effort after the funding stops and usually with much competition for these available funds.

The departments in the federal government are somewhat notorious, although understandably so, in generating far more applications than they can fund. By doing this they can demonstrate the need for their special funding, and perhaps get an increase in their allocation. This means that only a portion of the applicants receives the funds and many others feel that they have gone through a lot of work for nothing. But, don't throw that proposal away. Fine tune it, shop it around, and try again either to the same funding agency or to a different one. A good proposal is never wasted.

Perhaps the most ignored element of strategic thinking is the issue of time. It often takes longer to do a major program than was planned because there isn't a model that is complex enough to provide realistic time frames. A major building project, a major upgrading of the library system, or a referendum are projects that take a long time. While it is possible for the planning and construction management consultants to build an accurate timetable for construction and its companion tasks, it is difficult to predict elements that are political. Many projects have had negative press by promising a completion on a specific date without knowing all of the steps to get through the project. To be accurate the political and financial timelines need to be included. During the time that the project is underway, there may be a number of events outside your control that requires a contingency plan. A model for the steps needed to complete major projects is in Appendix A. It is only there to provide a starting point for you to use to research and document the various steps, costs, timelines, and responsibility for the task. You will need to get local estimates on the various steps and adjust the activities to your own situation.

In most libraries it takes at least one budget cycle to make a major change. The more complicated the political and financial agendas are the longer it takes and often this does not match up with the terms of the elected or appointed officials. This brings stress to the system. You may have to work with new mayors and other elected and appointed officials. Often the changes in the political leadership create barriers to success. In many communities, term limits require changing elected officials on a schedule. A cycle of a maximum of eight years per office means that there will be a constant parade of new officials. This situation emphasizes the need for a continuous process for a strategic view of the library development program. You should get legal authorization in legislation as early as possible in the process so that, as office holders change, they will see that the decision was already made by legislative bodies or voters and they will have to take specific counteraction to stop the project.

Planning should be cyclical and should be continuous. All public governmental authorities require some level of planning as part of their annual appropriation process. Usually it is a three-year cycle which is composed of last year's expenditures to provide a baseline for comparison, this year's expenditures to keep tabs on the flow of revenue and expenditures and to give indications whether the library will be within budget or not, and next year's projections for budgeting purposes. While management strategies change often and seem to have a flavor of the four-year cycle (related to the elections), there are some basics to virtually all of them. They usually include some planning effort, the creation of a mission and a vision, and the presentation of goals needed to attain the vision.

You can become buried in management acronyms such as Management By Objectives (MBO), Planned Program Budget System (PPBS), and other ones in fashion. Suffice it to say, that the only relevant fact to all this is that the library must be viewed as being well managed before it can become successful in fundraising.

The ability to tap the three sources for increasing funding (funds from taxes, funds from nontax revenues, and nonmonetary resources) is important to the development effort since each one of them has its advantages. Funds from taxes, while subject to politics and even political whims, tend to be stable over the long term, and generally speaking the same battles over the same issues are rare. It may have taken a major campaign to get computers, networking, and other tools for automation into the library the first time, but usually once it is in the budget, most cities will continue to support the expenditure for maintenance and upgrades. Unfortunately, they are often the most hide-bound funds. Their uses and spending tracking can often be quite stifling to any creativity in the public sector.

In spite of this, the payoff in increased funding for public libraries is almost always highest when it is local tax funds. Success in increasing local tax funds requires a long-term planned strategy. The most significant use of nontax funds is for strategic leverage, innovation, and as a change agent (Dowlin, 1989).

Funds from nontax revenues often provide a great deal more latitude in their use. On the other hand, you may have to raise them yourself and they usually require some kind of commitment on the part of the public library or the community for their expenditure. The library also must have the ability to receive the private monies or have support agencies that are legally recognized and are authorized to act on behalf of the library.

The third source is nonmonetary resources. While many libraries use volunteers from the community or donated services, they are often not quantified as financial resources. Voluntary efforts can provide many more hands and minds to accomplish tasks, but they do require management on the part of the librarians. A well-organized volunteer management program on the part of the library must be in place. Without orientation and guidance, all of their hard work may not be very effective.

The use of volunteers also often creates a group of enthusiastic advocates for the library. The ability to do this by the library leadership provides significant strategic payoff for the fundraising. The volunteers need to be trained, committed (a contract is important to spell out expectations by both parties), and rewarded for their work. Once the volunteers see advocacy as one of their volunteer responsibilities, it provides the library with significant advocacy power. Regardless of the source of funds, there are keys that are critical to sound management of the funds and program. They are strategic planning, accountability, communications, building the stakeholder constituency, and fostering innovation.

ALWAYS SELLING YOURSELF AND THE LIBRARY

Stay on your message regardless of what channel is being used. Your core message ties all of the communications together and should cover what you are (mission), what you want to be (vision), and the steps for getting there (goals and objectives). It is essential that the leadership stay focused on the commonly agreed message and incorporate it into all of your community relations efforts such as branding, your story, bumper sticker communications, firefighting situations, and if it happens, surfing the tsunami.

Use Creative Ways to Get Publicity

Increase your resources with pro bono consultants and volunteers. Check with your local or state advertising council. They often have a list of firms that are willing to provide your library with free or low cost consulting for branding or an ad campaign. Check with your TV, radio stations, and newspapers for free filler announcements. If they have some good jazzy clips that they can pop in and you have cultivated a relationship, you can get free advertising. Sometimes they will charge you for the space but usually will give you two for one or some kind of deal. An annual photography show with photos provided by the local news media is a good way to get media attention. With a reception funded by the Friends of the Library (FOL) or a merchant, you can get some of the media big wigs in the library. Having gallery space is helpful for creating new stakeholders such as the media and artists. You do need to have clear and legal policies over the management of the space.

Having meeting rooms for the public is also a way to get new stakeholders and to solidify relationships with current groups in the community. This space needs to be managed as well as the gallery space. Be aware of recent court cases that have limited the ability of the library to control who uses these spaces. The pendulum of control swings with the court rulings. At one time most libraries prohibited commercial, religious, or personal use of the common spaces, but then some courts ruled that if the library allowed anyone outside of the library to use the space they had to allow everyone. Recently the pendulum has swung back allowing libraries to place some reasonable restrictions in place. In all instances, have a good attorney draft or review any and all policies in this area.

If you check the American Library Association (ALA) Web sites and the state and local professional associations, you will see many creative ways for your library to get publicity that helps to generate outside funds. Check their publications, programs, and Web sites for ideas and how to do public relations events. The national and state associations also have conference programs and publications that can be very helpful.

KISS

This means "Keep It Simple Stupid." You need to have variations of your message and detailed back-up information, but the core message should be very simple. The challenge is that everyone wants to pile on their ideas and prejudices. Basically, you have three parts: strategic plan, implementation plan, and case statement.

Your *strategic plan* should be comprehensive in its scope but succinct in its message. It should contain the library's mission, vision, strategic goals to achieve the vision, and objectives to accomplish the goals. Your *implementation plan* should be management-focused statement of who, what, and when. All of those must be measurable and include benchmarks for success that work. Your *case statement* for increased funding should explain the short-term needs. The documentation should be attractive, induce people to read it, and provide the glue to hold all of the media offshoots together. Most of all it should be memorable and presentable.

Create a Must-Visit List

You should make a must-visit list of people and organizations that you need to cultivate. Make it a prioritized list and put the opportunities for cultivation on your calendar. Set a goal that you will touch base with local politicians, foundation leaders, corporate leaders, the FOL, and so on every so often. Some of these will be at another event. A meeting of the city council or community board is a preset opportunity. Just see who is there and make your list of whom you need to talk with during their breaks. Educate and cultivate.

SELLING WITH SIZZLE

Turn mundane events like budget hearings into presentations for the wider audience. Sometimes you might get a lot of coverage when you do something controversial even if you didn't plan it that way. Do show and tells with testimonials from happy library supporters in budget hearings. Demonstrate your new technology at political events.

Star Power

If you can make contact with celebrities (or sometimes their agents), many authors, movie stars, sports figures, and other known people will volunteer their time for library events. Sometimes, even when their agent turns you down, the star will go ahead and volunteer for your program if you can reach them directly. Julie Andrews is honorary chair of the ALA National Library Week for this year. Robert Redford, Amy Tan, Angela Allende, and Amistad Maupin have been free with their time to help library and reading causes. You probably have well-known authors, actors, or sports figures in your community. You might even want to get controversial speakers such as Gloria Steinem who started tongues wagging all over Wyoming and attracted a lot of attention for the library as a source of community dialogue.

The press relations staff of professional or college sports organizations are happy to provide well-known athletes to attend events. It is always good press when a large football or tall basketball player sits on a chair in the children's library and reads to some children.

LEVERAGING FUNDING

It is very logical to leverage funding to get more funding, but many librarians don't look at their fundraising activities in this way. If the FOL has a booksale and lets you spend the profits to market the library's needs to the community or create a stronger brand, the original funds will pay off more than by just buying books. Often funds are available for the planning part of the development process. This is often the first step to get the program underway. It is important that you define the need for funds, quantify it, and communicate it to your stakeholders. The starter events (Nibbles and Starter Recipes) in Chapter 5 are good starting points for funds that can be leveraged. Consider all of these activities as a progression and always keep this in mind for the strategic view.

BUILDING RELATIONSHIPS

It is critical that your approach to your community (especially communities in a large city) be based on exclusivity or differentiation from all of the other competing demands for their time or money. The ability to communicate is critical and if you can build positive relationships, your chance of having successful communications increases.

The key here is to provide the leadership and expertise to the community to assess the need, create the opportunity, and to manage the alliances. The success will come when the library has an excellent program for networking with the stakeholders. This networking needs to be targeted to the different segments of stakeholders, be up to date, accurate, and involve two-way communications. The online tools have a huge potential of personalizing the communications to groups and individuals far beyond what has been available prior to the Internet era. If you get stakeholders using or at least connected to the library, you have gone a long way toward a successful strategic development campaign. You must remember however, that you need a solid case statement and leadership support before you start the targeted communications. If your case statement is unclear, appears amateurish, or is nonexistent, the communication attempts will turn off the audience.

Community Connectedness

The most successful librarians are those who, in additional to their professional leadership, are most closely connected to their community. The perceptions and understandings of these connections can be considered as a community compact. It isn't usually written down and formally adopted, but it does help people to understand the historical relationship. Using it to set the stage helps explain to people the relationship among the different options for funding and services. This provides a rational approach to the community debate about funding issues such as the monies for implementing new services or programs. This relates to the view of the public that services that have been available without a user fee should continue to be provided by governmental funding. Since the public has been funding the functions of acquisition, organization, and managing a book collection for decades if not hundreds of years, the public generally expects that the city, county, district, or whatever political entity to provide adequate funding for that function. They may not provide enough to satisfy the staff, supporters, or users but the concept of the library having to raise funds to staff a circulation desk is a tough sell to donors. It is important to create at least a mental historic compact as you progress.

When you move outside of the historical compact such as introducing new services that are not mainstreamed, charging fees for convenience or soliciting donations to get new services started, you need to get the public's support for the increased cost or the reduction in an existing service to cover the increased cost. Examples are providing copying service. Few libraries provide that for free since it can lead to violations of copyrights, costs money for the machine and supplies, and is generally accepted that libraries don't offer free copying. Since cheap copies are available to people at places like Kinko's and other copy shops, the only rationale for having public copying available is convenience especially since some printed items cannot be removed from the library and protection of the items in the collection. Another example was online searching for databases twenty years ago. The early online databases were expensive, charged by the number of hits, pages, or articles on a per search basis and so few libraries provided access free at the start. With the new online databases, such service can easily be provided for free. The only charges might be for printing copies of documents the patrons wished to take with them.

John Gardner provided a great deal of thought to the issue of the creation or revitalization of community. A library can be one of the strongest agencies in a community for community building by providing a neutral institution with many resources to create or sustain a community. Libraries have places for people to meet, communication channels through their stakeholders, and can provide leadership to the effort. Both the ALA annual conference and the International Federation of Library Associations (IFLA) Congress in 2007 had several speakers who stressed the library as an institution important to communities.

BRING IN OUTSIDE TALENT TO THE PROJECT

Library directors don't need to know everything if they know how to find and pay for people who are skilled in a particular activity needed for library success. In libraries, directors routinely use experts as architects, planners, electricians, and others, but often overlook some of the other areas. With computers the librarian needs to hire or train staff that is knowledgeable in technology management and operation. Since you need a variety of consultants ranging from experts with setting up a library foundation to experts in getting signatures for the ballot proposition, this does require the librarian to have the skills for recruiting, contracting, and managing all of these different people or organizations.

People with Clout

It is a huge plus if you can find people who have respect, knowledge, motivation, and communication skills that will be champions for the library. Mrs. Astor was one for the New York Public Library. Mel and Charlotte Swing in San Francisco, and Bill Gates and Paul Allen in Seattle are outstanding examples of people who have these attributes and care for libraries.

When dealing with these people you need to be sure that you are accurate in your information, succinct and don't waste their time. Pay attention to their body language, keep their trust, and stay focused on your task. It helps if you attend social, political, or business events where they can get to recognize you and at least partially accept you into their sphere. Cultivate their relevant others, their staff, and their friends. If you can, become part of their inner circle. Sometimes it is just the little things. They will often bring the resources of their corporation, foundation, or other such organizations to assist in the project.

The vice president for creativity for Disney became very involved in the renovation and expansion for the Cerritos new main library project. The librarian and the staff worked with people to create the vision for each of the areas in the library and then used Disney artistic talent to create storyboards similar to cartoons showing the architects what each area should look like as a finished product. His effort helped expand the possibilities for public library status and capabilities well into the future.

People Who Care

While recruiting supporters for the library, you are fortunate if you can connect with people who are passionate about the library. Your primary challenge then is to get them to be involved in the vision and the effort to change the library. Sometimes their passion is for the library the way it was and that makes it very difficult to change to adjust to new needs and expectations in the community.

Other people who can be very effective are those people who are passionate about the community and who can be educated to understand the value of the library to the community now and in the future. Many philanthropists believe that they have the responsibility to give back to the community. The story of Andrew Carnegie's childhood when he became an ardent user and fan of libraries that led to his gigantic bequest is quite well known. This bequest stimulated thousands of libraries throughout the world.

Leadership for the affinity groups is also necessary. This effort should be led by people who care strongly about their community or cause, who can grasp that the library can help their dreams, and are willing to become avid supporters of the broader goals of the library.

Scout for Talent Outside Your Community

Another excellent way of adding outside talent is to check out other library's Web sites. It is free and can give you great ideas. Start with a list of the best current Web sites (Farkas, Website Design). Take a look at the Web sites of those libraries listed in the HAPLR index (Hennen, 2001). The link to Libraries Matter shows a very creative program at the Alliance Library System in East Peoria Illinois and Tumblebooks (Alliance Illinois Advocacy Day). The University of Pennsylvania has a great section for donors on their Web site (University of Pennsylvania). Another great site is the Winnipeg Library Foundation Campaign Web site (Winnipeg Library Foundation Campaign). You need to be careful about poaching on other people's talent pools, but looking at their lists of supporters might give you new ideas of types of people to recruit for your project.

POLITICAL SAVVY

Timing is critical when dealing with political organizations and individuals. You must do your homework in your personal development, development within the organization, financial management, and resource stewardship before you step on the stage of the big-time development. If you are well prepared, you have the ability to be opportunistic and creative. A strategic development program is a lot like building a snowman. First you must take some snow in your hand and shape it into a ball. After you get a big enough ball of snow, you put it in the snow on the ground and roll it down the hill. Eventually if you have enough snow, know how to make a snowman, and get lots of good help, you can build a great snowman. If you and your stakeholders are motivated, organized, and have a shared vision you can even build a snow fort or city.

At that point the challenge isn't getting people involved in the endeavor, but to decide which ones have the ability to add, not detract from reaching the vision. That is an art in itself. Ask any library director who has been successful in a major strategic development program and they will tell you that timing is critical. Understanding when the time is right to enter into a different phase or activity is very important. If your vision is revealed and it is way too grandiose to excite people, little will be accomplished. While vision is critical for success, it must be a creditable one as well as a shared one.

Nurturing Political Leaders

Cultivating political leaders is probably more an art than a science. Yet there are patterns that increase your chances for success. Find some of your supporters that have a good relationship with the elected or appointed official. If you can't find someone already in your stakeholder network, either find someone who is close to the official who you can educate to become an advocate or find someone with motivation and good communication skills who will work toward a relationship with the official. A natural starting point is to sort out all of the elected leaders in your community and assess their support for the library program. Start with the ones who are your friends or friends of friends. Develop a leader cultivation program. If your community has a program for the development of up-and-coming leaders, volunteer as well as offer your library's information and knowledge resources to the group. The better the information for elected officials, the better chance you have to succeed.

If you are starting to cultivate relations with officials, it is important to spend time with "newbie's." They often don't have their plate filled up with long-term commitments and attitudes. They tend to be more open-minded and willing to listen. If you can find someone with an allied interest such as education, reading, adult literacy, or community development, you have an improved chance for a good start. Remember that you need to have cleaned out your kitchen, organized it, and built your case for political action.

It was mentioned earlier how important it is for the director or other people associated with the library to get to know the aides and secretaries of important people. It often works well with the spouse or partner of an elected or appointed official as well.

Once you have made your roster of stakeholders who are officials and have assessed their probability of increased support, you need to find the communication channels that work. Sometimes it is just hanging around political events, providing a venue for political communications such as the Community TV Forums or finding someone who can get you in the door. Once you get in the door, make your case succinctly and persuasively. Have your facts in hand (or your head) and leave them something tangible to look at, but not until you are through speaking or they may start reading and not listening. Always have something to say to them when you have the opportunity. Get them personally involved if you can.

Invite all elected officials to library events. Have them introduce speakers at a program. Let them appear in your video productions and get their endorsements for any library issue that you can.

Different actions are needed before the person is elected and after they are elected. If they are one of several running for that office and they have not been elected, you need to invite all of the candidates to participate. If you have community political forums, invite all candidates for state, local, and federal office. But often you might have the governor or president of the senate attend functions after they are elected. You can usually get elected officials to do menial tasks at the opening of a new library. These occasions provide an opportunity to enlist them as supporters of the library. It offers candidates and elected officials the opportunity to meet most of the adults at the event, and it certainly gives the library a local political boost. This is all about connections.

While there may be prohibitions for your serving in some elected or appointed offices, you may have family members who are involved. Even with some restrictions on your participation for other reasons, this relationship allows you the opportunity to tag along to political events with someone else. Politicians are rational actors. They just sometimes have different goals than you do. But most of them are willing to listen, and if you have a good case, you can influence their opinion and actions.

Build a Constituency

Think in terms of converting your stakeholders into a constituency. Everyone in your community is a stakeholder in one way or another. A relationship to the library may be quite remote to some people because they don't use it. Part of the task is to convince them that they have a responsibility for the well-being of the library as well as part of living in a healthy community. Its future is not just determined by the elected or appointed officials. That future will be driven by the members of the community if they wish to do so. If they don't choose to do so, it is a failure on the part of the library leadership.

BUILD ON SUCCESS

Having small events and fundraising projects set the stage for the bigger endeavors. It is far easier to recruit collaborators and supporters if you have a reputation for being successful. It takes practice to pull off community-wide events. A relationship has to be nurtured and built among the library staff and supporters and the volunteers who are doing the programs. Many of the FOL volunteers who work on the annual or ongoing booksales are doing it because they enjoy being around the books, want the books to be recycled within the community, and have a camaraderie with other folks involved in the event. They should also be educated on the value of the booksale to the library and know the strategic vision and issues of the library. Some libraries have very successful booksales, but the organizers and volunteers of the booksale seem to be little interested in the library's overall needs. They have not been educated on the strategic vision, issues, and needs.

Once we have created an active organization and developed some ongoing programs to create some flexible seed money, it is time to go for bigger things. Remember the snowball effect. Use the money from the booksales to invest in talent for larger community relations and programming. Set up and publicize public programs using the talents of the authors or celebrities in the community. With just one event, some of the affinity groups can raise hundreds of thousands of dollars for a library foundation.

Some of these events are a bit speculative. The first time you have a particular event, you may not make much money. This is where the financial backing of the FOL, Foundation, or another support group is critical. It is rare that you can actually budget for public events such as receptions or celebrations in a publicly funded budget. Having that flexibility is critical for a successful development program.

Family Celebrations

Get your folks together anytime you can celebrate success and encourage them to further support. Good food, drink, music, and words thanking them for their help are always welcome. You may have to start small.

You should have events in the neighborhoods, at the branches, at county fairs, and any other place that you can get people together. Take your bookmobile or kidsmobile to the county fair along with an exhibit in the big tent.

Building a Reputation for Success

In your library you may find something called the "tipping point." This is a term that apparently originated as a scientific term relating to epidemics and perhaps if it is a bit grandiose to apply to libraries, it is instructive. As Gladwell states, "It's that ideas and behavior and messages and products sometimes behave just like outbreaks of infectious disease" (Gladwell). In more relevant terms, the library reaches the point where it has become a household name and image. This is a magical point where everything seems to work and everybody seems to be on board. It is difficult to quantify but you will know it when it happens.

LEVERAGING ASSETS

The successful fundraising includes a mixed revenues approach. You will start with finding starter funding, and you will find talent to help you. You must have conceptual visioning. In this way, you increase options for your library.

The Mixed Revenues Approach

A real key to success is to understand that there must be a mixed funding bag with the majority of the funds coming from the government agencies responsible for the services but should also include one-time funding for capital projects, infusion of new cash for change implementation and management, and the ability to raise funds from nonprofits, corporations, and individuals. A rich and healthy mixture of funding sources increases the options for the library.

Producing Proposals for Starter Funding

A good proposal has a high chance of getting funding; it is just a question of time and being in the right place at the right time. Get the seed money to hire a grant proposal writer, someone who has a good track record. Produce a proposal for your state library to do a benchmark survey of attitudes and interests of the citizens of your community. This survey can set the stage for garnering political and public support for the project.

Find the Talent

The most important asset of any organization—and libraries are no exception—is the talent of the people who work there and support it. An organization such as a library needs even more varied talents these days than ever before. Libraries need not only librarians, technical, and support people but also experts in a number of fields. A person's talent in an organization may be very unique; and the ability of the leadership to recognize, nurture, and work with talented people is critical to a program for development. The most successful organizations blend the talents of many people and recognize that one talent will often be different between two people. The ability to know books and recommend good reads and sources in printed items is different than being an expert in online searching. The ability to lead or direct FOL will be different than the ability to lead or direct a major campaign for an election issue or a major private funding drive.

With that knowledge you only have to be an expert in three areas: strategic planning, leadership, and spotting talent. If you can raise funds in a grant, you can hire people to leverage those monies into larger and larger amounts.

Conceptual Visioning

The visioning part for a library can be complicated because it involves so many people who are so different from each other. Communities have different goals; different communities within communities have different goals. But, it is possible to create a community library vision with guidance and talent from the library professionals, community leadership, and other stakeholders. Then it is possible to create the "soul" of the library and the physical manifestations of that vision. Once we have the vision then we can move to the next step, strategic thinking.

In retrospect, it seems that there were four major components to strategic thinking. They are

1. creating a collaborative institution,
2. shifting the organization culture to a real time world,
3. creating the neographic institution, and
4. creating the organization for systemic strategic planning (Dowlin and Shapiro, 1996).

A major issue arises in creation of the virtual library.

The issue of funding virtual library functions is critical for the long term. Virtual reference services abound although they are trending to be operated by large regional consortiums or nonprofits such as OCLC. While this expands the reach and efficiency of virtual reference services, it dilutes the local connection the library has to its user. Attention needs to be paid to this issue since the majority of funding for public libraries in the United States today comes from local sources. As the networked services of libraries become wider and wider, the connection between the users and the funders widens. The biggest challenge for the "virtual library" isn't the technology; it is the connection to the funders.

If you take a look at all of the innovative projects started by federal funding through state grants, they were quite successful as long as there was state or federal funding. However, they didn't last when that support went away. Most librarians will spend their political capital and energies supporting state and federal programs that provide support directly to their library. Many failures can be cited along with successes.

A good example of retaining the community connection is the Global Reference Network that was started by the Library of Congress in 1997. It now has about 2,000 library members worldwide. While it functions like a virtual reference center, the portal and nodes are still local. This approach allows the libraries to stay in the view of their virtual constituents (Global Reference Library).

CREATE A BUZZ

Libraries are certainly trusted public institutions and polls show that they are considered one of the most valued public organizations as well. Yet, moving the community from benign feelings of support to active advocacy is a challenge. People who have donated money or time to the library became stakeholders through their sense of proud ownership.

Schedule fun events that are celebrations of success. Two good examples are the end of summer reading program party and the annual celebration of success in the literacy program.

Start a tradition of having an end-of-program party every year. Children who achieve the goal for the reading are invited along with their family to celebrate their success. It can start out as a rather modest affair but it tends to grow and grow. Most of the entertainment and refreshments can be donated by businesses in the community and the FOL will usually underwrite and contribute to its costs. It should be a huge success as a culmination for the summer's activities for children and many adults who attend became strong supporters of the library.

An annual celebration of success in the library's literacy program is an excellent bonding venue. The party is funded by donations, the people who attend have tremendous testimonies about the difference the program made in their lives, and it is a joyful occasion. It will bring in many people in the community who would not even think of the library as a resource for them to achieve their life goals. Be sure and invite the politicians as well. National Library Week and Children's Book Week provide opportunities for small events at the library.

Other events should generate celebrations, too. Finding events to celebrate at the library may include anniversaries in the community, if not a library milestone; it may be a group that you want to have a relationship with the library. An example of these could be Founders Day for the community with many exhibits from the library's archives, or an exhibit at the county fair. As far as funding goes, a major campaign requires many celebrations along the way to mark various successes on the way to raising millions for furniture, fixtures, and equipment for the library or getting a referendum passed and implemented. The more visible and active the library is in the community the greater are the chances of getting attention. A good library will have a lot of attention ranging from long-term loyalties and support to interesting happenings that have just taken place.

MANAGING THE PROCESS

It is part of your job to manage the entire process. Learn to use some kind of project management tool, or get one of your staff members to learn a program and keep it up-to-date. Keep track of what has been completed as well as what is left to be done. There are three tasks in the fund development program that need priority: the communications program, the donor management program, and the decisions support program.

Communications Program

The first task for the librarian is to create a systemic communications program. All of the library's communications should be tied together around the core message. All printed material or online images should be coordinated to convey an image of a single organized library and brand. Some supporters may chafe at the bit at having procedures and policy to follow, but it is important that everyone who has a communication role, including staff on the service desks, becomes knowledgeable about the mission, vision, and goals and objectives of the library. One of the primary goals should be to present a unified dynamic brand to the public.

You should start with the Web and take the advice of Laura Blanchard from the University of Pennsylvania. The key lesson is that "libraries and other nonprofit organizations should move toward a 'wired' or Web-centric' communication mode." "Always start your communications with the web in mind" (Blanchard and Corson-Finnerty, p. 111). Much of the public relations material for libraries today is paper centric and the Web pages are simply static pages that were developed for print.

The result in this shift from paper to the Internet is often labeled Library 2.0. You can find a great deal of information on that concept on the Internet and in the most recent library literature. At the 2007 ALA conference, RUSA had a preconference titled Reinventing Reference 3. The keynote speech by Michael Stephens is an excellent list of the steps for success (Stephens). Another good source is the project done by Tom Peters for the Alliance Library System in Illinois (Alliance Library System Library 2.0).

One strategy to create a successful community relations and marketing program is to use funding from outside service grants to expand the Community Relations Office (CRO). Excellent adult literacy programs exist in libraries throughout California due to strong local interest, funding via the State of California and the Federal Government for development of new programs and the expansion of existing ones. The directors of these programs have become very good at recruiting volunteers for tutors and other activities, communicating with all of their stakeholders, and above all getting them together for "feel good" events.

If the library has received grants projects from agencies such as the National Science Foundation, the Institute for Museums and Library Services to provide demonstration projects, it is acceptable to include costs for publicizing these programs. The money can expand capacity by pooling the portion of the funds that are for publicity. For example, if you can get four different grants and each grant funds one-fourth of a person for the CRO, you can hire a full-time professional public relations person. Or if you get two grants that have one-fourth time position funds, you can request funds from you primary funding source for matching funds for the grants and achieve your goal. Many grants won't let you buy equipment with the grant money. You might need to get your computer equipment through a local foundation or community group. Once you have developed an excellent CRO from "soft" funding (most grants have an ending date for the funding) you can use its talent to cultivate stakeholders and to promote the library to the specific stakeholder groups.

It doesn't take a lot of money to get a talented Web manager and the payoff is exceptionally good. It is important to have staff with the skills for the new generation stakeholders so that you can create a powerful communication tool to cultivate stakeholders. One tool that has excellent potential is MyLibrary, which is discussed later.

Donor Management Program

The second task is to create a database that tracks donors. You need to keep track of people, money, and results in real time and to have regular reports on the status of meeting the goals for the campaign. The image used by United Way of a thermometer that moves up to the top is a good way of displaying progress. You also need good fundraising management software.

Eric Friedenwald-Fishman from the Metropolitan Group states that one of the important criteria for fundraising management software is that it should be appropriate to the scale of your campaign. Perhaps you will only need it for a limited number of donors or a short period of time, so you might not want to invest in a system with all the bells and whistles. You will also need to decide if you are going to use a program on your local computer or to use a network-based product (Friedenwald-Fishman, 2007). A number of systems are designed for fund development management campaign. Some of them are quite sophisticated but require specialized training for their implementation and operation. You can get a look at one of the products available at DonorPerfect that allows you to test drive the program before buying it (DonorPerfect). It may not be available through the normal library automation vendor programs, but the ideal system would be one that has the ability to identify donors and supporters through the user registration system that is part of the overall system. You need a system to protect the information you locate and store.

Care does need to be taken to protect the information from unauthorized use. It could be fantastic research tool as well as management information for a campaign. One of the tasks of this database should be to provide information as a Virtual Donor Wall on the Web site where any donor who desires it can be listed. This Wall should have a link directly from the home page under library supporters.

DECISION SUPPORT PROGRAM

The third task is to create a Decision Support System. The Decision Support System is one of the tools needed for good management of a library, and its utility should include a funding management component. It should be accurate, current, and provide relevant data for management decisions. Data should be shown in context and changes in levels of counts should be identified clearly.

MyLibrary

Yahoo and Amazon.com are perhaps the best-known businesses for developing a personalized Web site for the individual. The precepts displayed by those corporations influenced some academic libraries to undertake the development of MyLibrary. North Carolina State, creating theirs some seven years ago, seems to be the first one to develop the programs (NCSU, MyLibrary). Now the Virginia Commonwealth University, California Polytechnic State University, the University of Washington, and Notre Dame University have robust MyLibrary implementations. Perhaps the most sophisticated implementation is at Notre Dame University. Check out the NCSU MyLibrary at their Web site and take a look at the recent upgrade at Notre Dame. Notre Dame, which personalizes the Web site for the individual by providing linkages to other Web systems, has a marketing and partner focus, and is a trusted source of information.

Such an offering could be an outstanding tool for marketing the library and enlisting support groups such as the FOL. The individual should be offered a menu of personalized services and should be able to choose which functions they are interested in. Those with young children may be interested in having alerts e-mailed to them with a link to the program information. All kinds of clubs and interest groups could be linked through this service. The system could be used to collect information on the interests of the user as Amazon.com does. Based on that information, the site can become very personalized. It is imperative that the library adopt a user privacy policy, share that policy with all, and allow users to make choices about what information they will provide and what information they want to receive. Personalized reader guides, reading lists, search strategies focused on the age and education of the user, search and display preferences, and allow the user to ask reference questions, renew books, and other self-service functions. Linked with a credit card system, the user can pay fines and fees online.

Online book discussion groups can be set up composed of people who have common interests. The site could be linked to online book vendors if the user is interested in ordering items that the library does not have in their collection. The Free Software Foundation, Inc. will provide you with the free software. Check them out at http://dewey.library.nd.edu/mylibrary/LICENSE.shtml . The recent enhancement of the program by the University of Notre Dame appears to be an excellent starting template for a MyLibrary at a public library. You can take the core functions and start designing components that assist in the strategic funding program. But first let's define it for the average person.

Notre Dame and North Carolina State seem to agree on the basics that need to be included. According to a flyer that Notre Dame picks up from North Carolina State, "It is more than a just a portal, it includes a service allowing users to regularly receive and search lists of new books added to the library's collection, the Current Awareness service. Using Library of Congress call numbers for books and serials, users can create any number of Current Awareness profiles. Once you have the profiles provided by the user the system can alert the users about events and resources available to this user. Results are sent to a user's email address which allows direct access to the library catalog via a hotlink and to more information describing the resource or service." A thorough handbook listing all of the participants in the MyLibrary consortium group is available at http://mylibrary.library.nd.edu/documentation/ch/ch01.html.

OurLibrary

In considering the progress that has been made in personalizing Web sites or portals following the lead of the online shopping opportunities by corporations such as Amazon.com and Yahoo, personalizing the library's portal would be a good way to entice and connect new stakeholders to the library. You need to go beyond the concept of "my" in order to convince the stakeholders to support the library and the community-wide nature of libraries. MyYahoo is basically a transaction-based system where you give them something in return for their services. As it is called in the industry, they get "eyeballs" or "clicks" which they sell to get advertisers to pay them rather than ask the user for money. In return they give you a focused and personalized information source.

A major difference between a business operation and a library is that almost all libraries are about community. The community can be the faculty and staff at an academic institution, the public and users in a legal community such as a city or county, or the employees in a corporation. The library can't just be a library, or even MyLibrary.

The most successful libraries are seen as OurLibrary by the community. People like to participate in library programs and services and many would be active participants in the library's development if approached and educated as to the needs of the library. They need to be involved, participate, and asked to help. The library needs to create OurLibrary online. While there isn't a definitive design for OurLibrary, it should include certain elements.

It should have layered categories of users similar to the people who use the physical library. A person who walks in the door and uses resources in the building is in one category. This level of service is usually open to everyone in a public library building. The same category should apply to the online user. They should be able to use all of the resources that are online such as the catalog, which is available to everybody. Their services are limited since members of this category do not pay for these services via their tax funds. Think of them as tourists.

The next level is for people who have the ability to check out physical items from the library or receive a higher level of information or knowledge services than the tourist. This would include virtual services as well. Usually this requires some kind of registration process and requires the person to be a resident of the community that funds the library, have reciprocal relationships with their own library, subsidy by the state, or some other legal authorization. The FOL and Foundation members should be at the top level of the data system due to their commitment to supporting the library.

Another function of OurLibrary should be to provide the portal to the library's resources tailor-made for the user and a portal to the Internet world enriched by the expertise of the library staff. It should emphasize that the user, supporter, and all of the stakeholders should view their connection to the library as two-way. They need to understand that their help is needed for the future of the library and that they need to be involved with the library's future.

Some of the key attributes of OurLibrary is that it would be highly interactive with the stakeholder, should educate them about the library, offer opportunities to help the library by volunteering or donating money, creating shared goals with the stakeholders, provide interactive planning and surveys, and should start recruiting the young people in ways that are relevant to them. It should start when they register for borrowing privileges. They should be encouraged to register online from home or at the registration desk. Their card would be activated for borrowing privileges when they present a photo ID to library staff.

You should investigate the more current tools for library communication such as MySpace, SecondLife, and Mashups. They do appear to have potential to be an additional communication tool if integrated or linked to the core message and other information about the library. Each one should be assessed for its ability for extending communications and in creating new stakeholders. They will be important since the millennium generation use these tools as youth so they will probably continue to use them throughout their lives. You must incorporate them into their pattern of communication so that they relate to the library throughout their lives. Another example of this is also from North Carolina.

The Public Library of Charlotte and Mecklenburg County has a Virtual Village Communication Center (VVCC). Their pages for getting people and communities involved are outstanding. Their VVCC includes a Digital Darkroom, Music Composition, Video Editing, Adaptive &Assistive Technology Stations, Express Stations, Graphics Stations, Web Stations, and a Training Room. Their training classes are extensive and are a great way to build stakeholders (PLCMC). It would be interesting if the people taking the classes and using all of the tools in the Virtual Village can be converted to advocates for the library through the online links. A similar VVCC was available at the Public Library in Oslo, Norway, when IFLA held their conference there in 2006. It was very impressive because of the resources made available to members of the community.

As it grows in popularity, the virtual world of Second Life has potential for community communications involving the library. The San Jose State University's (SJSU) School of Library and Information Science (SLIS) now has a presence in Second Life and is exploring its use for educating librarians. Virtual libraries are also present on the site. Some of the normal services create stakeholders that have the ability to become outstanding supporters.

JUST DO IT

In summary, we should bring this book to a close with a bit of a review. The book focused on a strategic view that is created by library leadership with the involvement of as many library stakeholders as possible. It starts with knowing the community the library serves, building the organization to succeed, and executing the strategic development plan. If you can create a library with a soul, the library's successful future is assured. Our communities need institutions with souls in this time of constant, inevitable change. The library can be that institution. Its ability to archive the past, participate in the present, and prepare the community for the future is much stronger than any other institution that is open to everybody. This library is committed to success, central to their stakeholders, and connected to their community. The soul of a library comes from the people who are stakeholders; those people who value, use, and support the library in its many manifestations.

Appendix

This section contains three illustrations to provide a starting point for discussions for your planning meetings. They are:

A Visual Map that is designed to show the complex linkages with the various support groups. Balancing the communication and activities of the process can be very complex. The groups distance from the center (the Director) is to indicate the priorities of the communication and education effort. The most important linkage in any environment that is political is your boss. They must be knowledgeable, or trusting in what your aspirations and goals are for the library. This is further complicated by the fact that in a public institution the political leadership can change quickly. A new mayor, university president, or board of trustees must be brought into the process. It takes time and focus to bring them up to speed and it is your responsibility to do so. Failure to do so can be costly, time consuming, and may totally stall the project.

VISUAL MAP OF WORKING RELATIONSHIPS

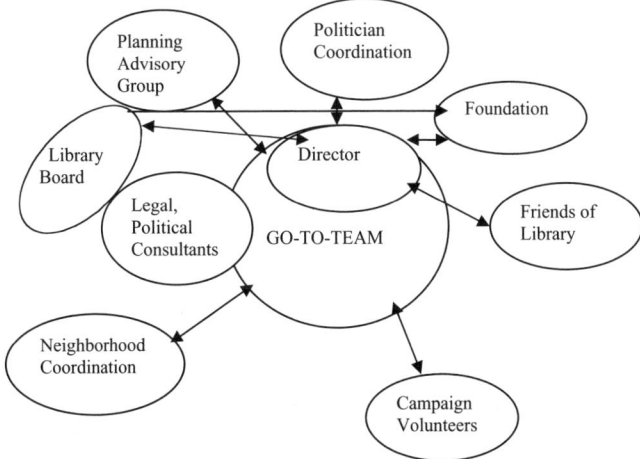

GETTING THE MONEY WORKSHEET

Activity	Duration	Participants	Estimated Costs[a]		Potential Source of Funding	Estimated Start Date
Planning and organizing	12 months duration					
Initial vision building	3 months	Director, staff leadership team, support group leaders	5,000	Supplies, meeting costs	FOL, community organizations, IMLS, angel[b]	Day 1
Create or invigorate FOL, and other support groups	12 months	Director, staff leadership, governing board	5,000	Publicity, membership and leadership development	Community foundation, community organizations, angel	Day 1
Create your Go-to-Team	3 months	Director, staff leadership team, support group leaders, angel, a political leader	2,000	Communications, miscellaneous		Day 5
Strategic plan	18 months	Director, staff leadership team, support group leaders, political rep., angel(s)	150,000	Consultants, miscellaneous	FOL, parent govt., IMLS, community foundations, corporate donors	+8 months
Benchmark survey	6 months	Consultants	50,000	Consultant, miscellaneous	Grants, FOL, parent govt.	+8 months
Develop long-term financial needs estimate	6 months	Director, staff leadership, consultant	50,000	Research, consultant	FOL, grants, community foundations	+24 months

130

Activity	Duration	Responsibility	Cost ($)	Expenses	Funding Sources	Timing
Start seed money fund raising activities	30 months	FOL	5,000	Organizing, training, communications	FOL, community foundations, corporate marketing departments	+6 months
Expansion of community relations office	24	Director, governing board	200,000	Staffing, technology, training	Regular budget, FOL, Foundation, grant publicity components	+6 months
Stakeholder development program	36 months	Director, staff leadership team, support group leaders, political rep., angel(s)	100,000	Publicity, communications program, events	Regular budget, grants, donations	+6 months
Relationship cultivation program	36 months	Director, staff leadership team, support group leaders, political rep., angel(s)	5,000	Miscellaneous	Regular budget	+12 months
Create platforms for communications	6 months	CRO	5,000	Publicity		
Create our library portal	12 months	Library budget, FOL, grants	35,000	Staff, consultant	Library budget, grant publicity components	+6 months
Create neighborhood group communications program	6 months	Staff leadership, political rep., neighborhood leaders or organizers	5,000	Meeting expenses	Community foundations, state library, local organizations	+12 months (overlaps SP)

(Continued)

Activity	Duration	Participants	Estimated Costs[a]		Potential Source of Funding	Estimated Start Date
Political support campaign	18 months	Director, staff leadership team, support group leaders, political campaign committee	5,000	Miscellaneous	FOL, library leadership	+12 months (overlaps SP)
Parent organization value added projects	36 months	Director, library staff, volunteers	0		Library budget, grants, governing agency budget	+6 months
Private fundraising[c]	36 months total					
Find seed money	6 months	Director, staff leadership team, support group leaders, political rep., angel(s)	50,000	Planning, legal work,	FOL, community foundations, angel	+1 month
Create library foundation	12 months	Director, staff leadership team, support group leaders, political rep., angel(s)	25,000	Consultant, legal work, financial setup	Community foundations, FOL, angel, library leadership	+12 months
Hire consultant	3 months	Director, Foundation Board	5,000	Interview expenses	FOL, foundation seed money	+6 months
Hire staff, set up office	6 months	Foundation Board	< 6 % of total raised	Operations	Foundation budget	+6 months

Set up donor management program	3 months	Foundation	15,000	Consultant, software, hardware	FOL, foundation	+10 months
Create case statement	3 months	Foundation Board, director	15,000	Research, writing, publication	Foundation budget	+3
Research potential donors	6 months	Foundation staff		Research	Foundation budget	+6 months
Locate and recruit campaign chair(s)	3 months				Foundation budget	+6 months
Start fundraising campaign	1 week	Foundation Board, staff, and other supporters	50,000	Publicity, solicitations	Foundation seed money	+8 months
Cultivate relationship for major donors to lead to sales meeting	12 months +	Foundation Board, staff, Go-to-Team	5,000	Communication	Foundation budget	+4 months
Political campaign[c]	24 months +					
Set goals for political campaign	3 months	Library leadership	1,000	Research, meetings	FOL	Day 1
Feasibility study for political campaign	6 months	Consultants	25,000	Consultant fees and expenses, legal research	Community foundations, FOL	+2 months

(Continued)

Activity	Duration	Participants	Estimated Costs[a]		Potential Source of Funding	Estimated Start Date
Establish campaign team	6 months	Director, staff leadership team, support group leaders, political rep., angel(s), legal advisers, financial advisors, campaign consultation, fundraiser	10,000	Team building, communications	FOL, foundation, political supporters	+2 months
Raise initial seed money	12 months	FOL, Foundation Board, angels	50,000	Communications, solicitations	Campaign team	+2 months
Estimate of strategic funding needs	3 months	Financial advisors, campaign consultant	25,000	Research, analysis	Campaign team	+6 months
Hire campaign consultant	4 months	Campaign team	120,000	Planning, campaign activities	Seed money	+8 months
Development of campaign statement	3 months	Director, FOL, Foundation, Governing Board, consultant	15,000	Research, writing, publications	FOL, foundation	+10 months
Start election campaign	12 months	Campaign committee	25,000	Campaign expenses	Campaign fund	+12 months
Polls	24 months	Polling organization	25,000	Polling	Campaign fund, foundation	+12 months
Endorsements	12 months	Campaign team	5,000	Solicitations, printing	Campaign fund	+12 months

Activity	Time	People	Cost ($)	Other resources	Funding source	Start
Expand volunteer pool	24 months	Campaign team, FOL, library volunteers	5,000	Communications	Campaign fund	+18 months
Speakers bureau expansion	12 months	Staff leadership, political rep., neighborhood leaders or organizers	5,000	Publicity, training	Grants, FOL	+18 months
Telephone banks	3 months	Volunteers	15,000	Spiel creation, telephone costs	Campaign fund	+20 months
Door-to-door campaigning	3 months	Volunteers		Publicity material	Campaign fund	+20 months
Countering opposition plan	12 months	Leadership	2,000	Publicity	Campaign fund	+10 months
Keeping up the enthusiasm	Life of campaign	Leadership	20,000	Communications, celebrations	Campaign fund, event donors	+18 months
Analyze for next time	3 months	Campaign team, consultant			Campaign fund	+25 months
Thanks all around	1 month	Campaign team			Campaign fund	+24 months

[a] All estimates of cost and time depend on local costing using experts for guidance. The numbers here are only to show relative scale for each activity.
[b] It can take a long time to find an angel, but get one as soon as you can.
[c] The campaign and private fund drive are treated as separate activities and can be started at different times. It is good to maximize the sharing of resources and activities when possible. For example, the media campaign should be coordinated by the library's Community Relations Office and director.

A worksheet that is designed to serve as a starting point for a to-do-list, a timeline, or a template for estimating the time the project will take. It is organized in sequence although there may be overlaps from time to time. If you adopt such a model it is recommended that you retain flexibility to adjust timelines as you go. Sometimes the initial time frame isn't much more than an educated guess. Estimates in your locale may vary widely in another. They are only starting points and care must be taken to ensure plenty of cushions for some part of it taking longer. Airline flights have significantly improved their on time arrival statistics by inflating the amount of time for the flight when it is scheduled. This model is an excellent communication tool to track accomplishments, make it clear what needs to be done, and who is responsible for getting it done. It should be revised regularly with every revision identified, dated, and showing the author of the update. Sophisticated planning tools can be used for this process and will make a much more comprehensive presentation document with its tables and timelines.

A checklist that is designed to be used to provide a scorecard for activity accomplishment and a tracking record for tasks to be done and those completed.

CHECKLIST FOR DEVELOPMENT OUTLINE

Phase I: Planning and Organization

> Who are you?
> Where do you want to go?
> How do you get there?
> How do you know you are making progress?

Strategic Planning

- ✓ Mission
- ✓ Vision
- ✓ Goals and objectives
- ✓ Measurements and benchmarks

Phase II: Implementation
Create stakeholders who will work for your vision

- ✓ Share your vision
- ✓ Setup communication channels
- ✓ Involve stakeholders
- ✓ Create a vision for the community

Create stakeholder organizations

- ✓ Friends of the Library
- ✓ Foundation
- ✓ Advisory councils

- ✓ Neighborhood groups
- ✓ Staff
- ✓ Funders (grants)

Create core leadership teams

- ✓ Go-to-Team
- ✓ Friends of the Library
- ✓ Foundation
- ✓ Policy body

Create platforms for communications

- ✓ Neighborhood budget hearings
- ✓ Community clubs and organizations
- ✓ Newsletters, flyers, etc.
- ✓ Web site
- ✓ OurLibrary
- ✓ Political events and celebrations
    - ➢ Cross paths with politicians
- ✓ Brand advertising
- ✓ Consistent organization image
- ✓ Program marketing
- ✓ Celebrations
- ✓ Recognition for supporters

Listen to stakeholders

- ✓ All of them, not just the ones with the loud voices

Involve stakeholders

- ✓ Ask them to help

Listen to your customers
Cultivate relationships

- ✓ Politicians
- ✓ Grants people
- ✓ Potential donors
- ✓ Talent

Leverage resources

- ✓ Collaboration
- ✓ Zero Sum Game (not)
- ✓ Congruent Goals
- ✓ Politics
- ✓ Technology

Add value to parent organization

- ✓ County Records system
- ✓ Cable casting, video capabilities
- ✓ Legal depositions in Wyoming
- ✓ Videos for hospitals
- ✓ Support education and learning
- ✓ Technology trail blazing

Bibliography

AALL. http://www.plan.gs/Article.do?orgId=935&articleId=7164.
AARP Bulletin. July–August 2007, p. 8.
ADA. http://www.usdoj.gov/crt/ada/adahom1.htm.
ALA. http://ALA.org.
ALA Blog. http://blog.alaeditions.org/2007/03/20/keeping-the-small-library-afloat-takes-planning/.
ALA OITP. http://iis.syr.edu/projects/PNOpen/ParticiaptoryNetworks.pdf.
ALA Washington Office. http://www.ala.org/washoff.
Alliance Illinois Advocacy Day. http://www.alliancelibrarysystem.com.
Alliance Library Network Second Life. http://www.alliancelibrarysystem.com.
Alliance Library System Advocacy Training. http://www.alliancelibrarysystem.com.
Alliance Library System Library 2.0. http://www.alliancelibrarysystem.com.
Bailey, Anne Lowrey. A Library's Appeal: Not by the Book. From the July 12 1994 issue of *The Chronicle of Philanthropy*, Copyrighted by the Chronicle of Higher Education, Inc. Posted with permission on Urban Parks Online, http://www.pps.org/topics/funding/fundstrat/libraryappeal.
Binder, David. http://www.davidbinderresearch.com/.
Blanchard, Laura. http://www.fund-online.com/.
Blanchard, *Laura and Adam Corson-Finnerty*. http://books.google.com/books?id=CfRMbNEfenAC&printsec=titlepage&dq=library+fund+raising.
Bolhassan, Rashidah. http://209.85.165.104/custom?q=cache:38va9y2HBVAJ:www.ifla.org/IV/ifla73/papers/128-Bolhassan-en.pdf+bolhassan&hl=en&ct=clnk&cd=1&gl=us.
Broady-Preston. 2007. http://209.85.165.104/custom?q=cache:58Gz8Zr1dbcJ:www.ifla.org/IV/ifla73/papers/158-Broady-Preston-en.pdf+Broady&hl=en&ct=clnk&cd=1&gl=us.
Bruijnzeels, Rob. Libraries 2044. http://www.splq.info/issuehttp://www.davinciinstitute.com/page.php?ID=120s/vol35_4/02.htm.
Coca Cola. 1969. The "Hilltop" Ad: The Story of a Commercial, http://memory.loc.gov/ammem/ccmphtml/colaadv.html.

Dempsey, Lorcan. http://www.oclc.org/research/staff/dempsey/dempsey_recombinant_library.pdf.

DonorPerfect. http://www.donorperfect.com/asp/info.asp.

Dowlin, Kenneth. 1989. "Fundraising—The Public Library Experience." *Library Administration and Management*. Spring Issue.

———. 2004. *The Library as Place: Challenges in the Digital Age. Libraries as Places: Buildings for the 21st Century*. Munchen, Germany: K.G Saur.

Dowlin, Kenneth and Lynn Magrath. 1983. "Beyond the Numbers—A Decision Support System." In *Library Automation as a Source of Management Information*, Wilfred Lancaster, ed., pp. 27–58. Champaign-Urbana, IL: University of Illinois Press.

Dowlin, Kenneth and Eleanor Shapiro. 1996. The Centrality of Communities to the Future of Major Public Libraries. *Daedalus*. Fall 1996. 185–188.

Dowlin, Kenneth and Marilyn Hope Smulyan. 1993. "Library Bond Campaigns". In *Against the Odds*, Linda Chrismond, ed., pp. 47–61. Fort Atkinson, WI: Highsmith Press.

Evans, G. Edward, Ward, P., and Rugaas, B. 2000. *Management Basics for Information Professionals*. New York City: Neal-Schuman Publishers.

Farkas, Meredith. "Balancing the Online Life." *American Libraries*. January 2007, 43.

———. "A Roadmap to Learning 2.0." *American Libraries*. February 2007, 26.

———. Website Design, http://www.libsuccess.org/index.php?title=Website_Design.

———. Wiki on Library Success, http://www.libsuccess.org/index.php?title=Main_Page.

Ferguson, Linda. http://www.niso.org/news/events_workshops/stat-webogr.html.

Fresno State University. http://www.csufresno.edu/.

Frey, Thomas. The Future of Libraries: Beginning the Great Transformation, http://www.davinciinstitute.com/page.php?ID=120.

Friedenwald-Fishman, Eric. Metropolitan Group presentation at ALA conference 2007.

Gardner, John W. http://www.pbs.org/johngardner/.

Giesecke, Joan. 1998. *Scenario Planning for Libraries*. Chicago, IL: ALA.

Gladwell. http://www.gladwell.com/tippingpoint/index.html.

Global Reference Library. http://www.loc.gov/rr/digiref/.

Goggin, Margaret Knox. Speech presented at the Isabel Nichol Lecture, May 24, 1984. Denver, Colorado.

Hennen, Thomas J., Jr. "Do You Know the Real Value of Your Library?" *Library Journal*, June 15, 2001, 48–59.

Holt, Glen. http://www.slpl.lib.mo.us/using/valuationtoc.htm.

Horan, Thomas. A New Civic Architecture: Bringing Electronic Space to Public Place, http://www.informaworld.com/smpp/content~content=a713684115~db=all.

IMLS. http://www.imls.gov/index.shtm.

Institute for Politics. http://www.apsanet.org/~itp/v2n3.pdf.

IRS. http://www.irs.gov/publications/p557/ch03.html#d0e7391.

Kanawha County Library. http://www.kanawha.lib.wv.us/building/case.html.

Kidder, Tracy. 2000. *Soul of a New Machine*. New York: Little, Brown and Company.

Kirkpatrick, Chad, and Tom Jenney. April 21, 2007. "Four Steps You Can Take to Bring Property Taxes under Control." *East Valley Tribune*, Commentary section, A19.

LAMA, fundraising and financial development section, http://www.ala.org/ala/lama/lamacommunity/lamacommittees/publicrelationsb/publicrelations.htm.

Laura. Keeping the Small Library Afloat Takes Planning. http://blog.alaeditions.org/2007/03/20/keeping-the-small-library-afloat-takes-planning/.

Mail and Guardian Online. http://www.mg.co.za/articlePage.aspx?articleid=299983&area=/budget07_home/budget07_insight/.

Mason, Robert and Tabatha Hart. 2007. *Libraries for a Global Networked World: Toward New Educational and Design Strategies.* WLIC 73rd IFLA General Conference and Council, Durban, South Africa.

Matthews, Joseph. 2007. *The Evaluation and Measurement of Library Services.* Englewood, CO: Libraries Unlimited.

Metropolitan Group. http://metgroup.com.

Metropolitan Group. www.metgroup.com/libraries.

Metropolitan Group Case Statement. http://www.metgroup.com/content/index.php?pid=102.

Mid-Hudson. http://midhudson.org/funding/fundraising/grantmakers.htm#program.

Minnesota Council of Nonprofits. http://www.mncn.org/doc/casestatement.pdf.

North Carolina State University (NCSU), MyLibrary. http://www.lib.ncsu.edu/mylibrary/about.html.

Notre Dame University. http://mylibrary.library.nd.edu/about-mylibrary.

NYLA. http://www.nysl.nysed.gov/libdev/.

OCLC. 2005. Perceptions of Libraries and Information Resources: A Report to the OCLC Membership. Dublin, OH: OCLC.

OCLC. 2007. Blended Learning. http://www.oclc.org/news/releases/200661.htm.

Ontario. http://www.culture.gov.on.ca/english/culdiv/library/lsdf.htm.

Placentia Library. http://www.plan.gs/Home.do?orgId=5311.

PLA TOOLKIT. www.alastore.ala.org.

PLCMC. http://plcmc.org/Locations/mainVirtualVillage.asp.

Poderis, Tony. http://www.raise-funds.com/library.html.

PPLD Grant. *Library Hotline*, June 18, 2007, 5.

Rund, Charles and Kevin O'Donnell. 1988. *San Francisco Public Library Citizen Attitude Survey March 1988.* San Francisco, CA: Charlton Research Company.

Second Life Wiki. http://www.simteach.com/wiki/index.php?title=Second_Life_Education_Wiki.

SFPL budget. Data tabulated by the California State Library from annual reports from SFPL filed with the state. Provided by e-mail to author on June 6, 2007.

Shafer, Scott. 1996. Author's notes from library workshop.

Southbury Public Library Junior Friends. http://www.biblio.org/Southbury/children/jrfriends.htm.

Steinbruner, John D. 1974. *The Cybernetic Theory of Decision, New Dimensions of Political Analysis.* Princeton, NJ: Princeton University Press.

Stephens, Michael. June 2007. http://alreadygone.blogspot.com/2007/06/reinventing-reference-3-keynote-by.html.

St. Mary's. 2007. http://www.washingtonpost.com/wp-dyn/content/article/2007/07/01/AR2007070100476.html.

The State of America's Libraries. A Report of the American Library Association. Chicago, IL: ALA. 2007.

Toronto Public Library. http://www.torontopubliclibrary.ca/sup_index.jsp.

Tufts Massachusetts Campus Compact. http://ase.tufts.edu/macc/creativetensions-learning.htm.

UCLA. http://www2.library.ucla.edu/development/1675.cfm.

University of Notre Dame, My Library flyer. http://dewey.library.nd.edu/mylibrary/.

University of Pennsylvania. http://www.library.upenn.edu/portal/benefactors.htmln.edu/portal/.

Urban Library Institute. Making Cities Stronger. http://www.urbanlibraries.org/files/making_cities_stronger.pdf.

Van House, Nancy and Stuart A. Sutton. 2000. "The Panda Syndrome: An Ecology of LIS Education." *Journal of Education for Library and Information Science*. Winter 2000, 53–68.
WebJunction, fundraising. http://webjunction.org/do/Navigation?category=404.
WebJunction, template. http://webjunction.org/do/DisplayContent?id=1500.
Winnipeg Library Foundation Campaign. http://www.millenniumlibrary.com/index.cfm.
Wyoming Library Roundup. http://www-wsl.state.wy.us/roundup/Win2007Roundup.pdf.
Wyoming State Library. http://www-wsl.state.wy.us/slpub/foundations/.
YALSA blog. http://blogs.ala.org/yalsa.php.
Yiotis, Krystin. Advocacy @ Your Library. March 4, 2007, PLA blog. Retrieved March 18, 2007, http://plablog.org/2007/03/advocacy-your-library-workshop.html.
Zaslow, Jeffrey. Of the Places You'll Go, Is the Library Still One of Them? *Wall Street Journal*. March 15, 2007, D1.

Index

Advocacy, 56–57, 59–61
Affinity group, 63, 92, 96, 118, 120
Alamogordo Public Library (NM), 103
ALA Trustees Association (ALTA), 53
Alliance Library Network, 67
Amazon.com, 75, 85, 125
American Association for Law Libraries (AALL), 80
American Libraries, 29, 101
American Library Association (ALA): Director of Consultants, 106; Freedom to Read Foundation, 86; on growth of electronic sources, 7; Handbook on Advocacy, 61; Office of Information Technology Project, 36; professional ethics and, 26; Washington Office, 82; Web site, 60; Web site, fundraising sources on, 68–69
American Public Library Ratings Index, 16, 23
Americans with Disability Act (ADA), 37

Anecdote, as communication tool, 63
Angels, 43, 47, 94
Antiquarian Book Dealers Association, 83–84
Ashes of deceased, interring at library, 83
Assets, leveraging, 121–22
Australia, 100
Authority issues, 28

Bagdikian, B., 92–93
Balanced Scorecard Methodology, 16
Baseball game fundraiser, 77
Bellingham Public Library (MA), 77
Bequests and wills, 79–80
Bill and Melinda Gates Foundation, 60, 89, 95
Blanchard, L., 124
BoatMobile, 8
Bond Act Funding (CA), 81
Bond issues, 99–100
Book fair, sponsored, 74
Bookmobile, 58, 64, 121
Bookplate, memorial, 75
Booksale, 73–74, 115, 120
Boston Public Library, 85

Boulder Colorado Public Library, 75
Branding, 47, 57, 58–59
Brick, memorial, 75
Brigham City Library (UT), 101
Bruijnzeels, R., 6–7
Budget: Planned Program Budgeting, 17; reducing personnel, 35; Zero Based Budgeting, 17
Bumper Sticker Communication, 25, 26, 57
Bumper Sticker Slogan, 23

Cable Television Systems (CATV), 66, 67, 76
California, state funding in, 81
California Association for Research Libraries, 81
California Library Association, 61
California Regional Library Systems, 45
California State Library, 9, 45
Carnegie Public Library, 85, 91
Case statement, 22–23, 115
CD/DVD, as communication tool, 68

Celebrities, 84, 96, 115, 120
Cerritos Public Library (CA), 37–38, 90–91, 117
Challenge/matching gift, 85, 93–94
Chamber of Commerce, 46, 90
Change, experiential library, 37–38; fortress to pipeline, 38; gatekeeper to facilitator, 38; government mandates, 34, 36; graphic to neographic content, 34–35; in libraries, 34–39; increase in access points, 35; Internet, 39; licensing and copyright, 36; managing, 41–42; ownership to access orientation, 36; self-service, 37; single to many simultaneous users, 35; singular to collaborative organizations, 36; singular to mass processes, 35; specific actions for librarians, 38–39
Charitable planned giving, 79–80
Charter City, 33
Checklist, for development outline, 136–38
Children's Book Week, 123
Children's center, public view of importance, 9
Closed *vs.* open system, 48–49
Colorado, state funding in, 81
Colorado Digitization Project, 46
Colorado Springs. *See* Pikes Peak Library District (PPLD)
Colorado Trust, 96
Commercial approaches, 82–86; creative project, 83–84; credit card program, 82, 86; interring ashes of deceased, 83; online fundraising, 84–86; transit company, 82–83
Communications program, 123–24

Communication skills: listening skills, 22, 24; presentations, 25–26; storytelling, 27. *See also* Communication tools
Communication tools, 51–52, 56; advocacy, 57, 59–61; Alliance Library network, 67; anecdotes, 63; branding, 57, 58–59; Bumper Sticker Communication, 25, 26, 57; Cable Television Systems (CATV), 66, 67, 76; CDs/DVDs, 68; commercial radio and television, 66; flyers/bookmarks/posters, 63–65; Internet (*see* Internet); marketing, 57; MyLibrary, 68, 75, 124–26; podcasts, 67; press releases, 64–65; print media, 65–66; public radio and television, 65; public relations, 56–57, 61–62; Second Life, 67, 128; testimonials, 62–63
Community building, as major marketing campaign theme, 92–93
Community foundations, 96–97
Community organization presentations, 72–73
Community organizations, 29–30
Community relationships, 116–17
Community Relations Office, 44, 52–53, 64, 68, 124
Community Resource Office, 99
Community survey, 8–10
Compliments and Complaints forms, 29
Comprehensive Employment and Training Act (CETA), 42
Conceptual visioning, 122
Connecticut Public Library, 55
Constituency building, 120

Contra Costa County Library, 85
Control system, clarifying and codifying, 18
Cookbook, as fundraiser, 74
Copyright, 36
Corporate/business approach, 94
Credit card program, 82, 86
Cultural institution partnership, 78

Danville Public Library, 90
Decision support program, 125–28; MyLibrary, 125–26; OurLibrary, 126–28
Decision Support System, 16, 77
Dempsey, L., 39
Denver Public Library, 85
Devils, 47–48
Dewey Decimal Classification System, 35
Direct mail campaign, 80
Director of Consultants (ALA), 106
Diversity, as major marketing campaign themes, 92
Doctrine of first use, 36
Donor management program, 124–25
DonorPerfect, 125
Donor recognition, 74–75
Door-to-door campaigning, 108–9
Dowling, M., 69
DVD/CD, as communication tool, 68

E-book, 35
Effectiveness and efficiency, assessing, 15–17
Elected officials: and bond issues, 99, 102–3; contributions from campaign fund of, 105, 107–8; cultivating, 119; cultivating aides and office personnel of, 49; educating about library, 24–25; and federal funding, 82;

identifying and reaching, 28–29; and local referendums, 97–98; muscle people, 47
End of summer reading program, celebrating success of, 123
Endowments, 80
Equipment donation, 76, 94
Evans, E., 45
Experiential library, 37–38
Experts, outside, 117
External organization development, 48–50; neighborhood organization alliances, 50; new stakeholders, 49; stakeholder alliances, 49–50

Fair Labor Standards Act, 37
Family celebration, as funding source, 82, 120–21
Family foundations, 96
Farkas, M., 10, 41, 93, 104
Feedback, 18
Ferguson, L., 16–17
Financial limitations, on funding, 32–33
Financial management, 27–28
Fines, overdue, 78
Flyers, 52, 63–65, 82
Formal support groups, 48, 53–56. *See also* Friends of the Library (FOL)
Fort Vancouver Library District (WA), 101
Foundation grants: small community, 78
Freedom to Read Foundation (ALA), 86
Free Software Foundation, Inc., 126
Frey, T., 38–39
Friedenwald-Fishman, E., 125
Friends of the Library (FOL), 22, 27–28, 33, 48; funding for referendum campaign, 108; nonlibrarian staff scholarship funding, 43; overview, 53–54; silent auctions and booksales, 74, 120
Friends of the Library USA (FOLUSA), 53, 60
Funding myths, 12; government funding, 13–14; nongovernment funding, 14–15

Gardner, J., 93, 117
Gates Foundation, 60, 89, 95
Giesecke, J., 42
Ginsburg, A., 31–32
Gladwell, 121
Global Reference Network, 122
Goggin, M.K., 88
Golf tournament fundraiser, 77
Goods donation, 94
Google, 1, 35, 68, 84, 89, 96, 100
Go-To-Team, 43–44; community members as part of, 44; elected and appointed officials as part of, 44–45; Internet as communication tool and, 68; loyal staff as part of, 44; project grant creator as part of, 45; and referendums, 103–4
Government agency partnership, 79
Great Bay Area Library Council (GBALC), 44–45
Great Books, 74
Group communications audit, 23–24

Harold Washington Main Library (Chicago), 91–92
Hennen, T., 16, 23
Hennepin City Library (MN), 85
Holt, G., 103
Horan, T., 39

Illinois Library Association, 60–61
Implementation plan, 114–15
Inadequate funding, primary reason for, 5
Indiana Public Library Board, 54–55
Inflation, effect on funding, 5
Institute for Politics, 96–97
Institute of Museum and Library Services (IMLS), 29, 46, 78, 96
Internal Revenue Service (IRS): on family-controlled foundations, 95; on lobbying, 54; nonprofit organization code, 33
International Federation of Library Associations (IFLA), 7, 60, 100, 117
Internet: booksales on, 74; as communication tool, 66–68; effect on libraries, 39; fundraising sources on, 68–69; online book discussion, 126; online fundraising, 84–86, 96–97
Internet Public Library, 61
Investment funds, 5

Jamaican National Library, 7
Journal access, 36
Journal/magazine subscription, donated, 75–76
Junior FOL, 48, 55

Kanawha County Public Library (WV), 104
Kidsmobile, 121
Knowledge and skills development, 21–22
Knowledge Index, 8

Lapsit programs, 76
Leanardo DeCaprio Charitable Foundation, 96
Learning 2.0, 41
Learning organization, creating, 40–41
Lehigh University, 103
Leveraging funding, 115–16
Lexington Public Library, 65
Librarian: as manager, 12–13; myth about need for, 12

INDEX

Librarianship, defining, 57
Libraries for the Future, 60
Library: defining, 57; shifting role of, 30
Library 2.0, 124
Library Administration and Management Association (LAMA), 69
Library and Information Science (LIS), 7, 46
Library Foundation, 22
Library foundation: and major capital campaigns, 96; overview of, 54–55
Library of Congress, 122
Library of Congress Classification System, 35
Lifelong learning, 24
Listening skills, 24
Literacy program, celebrating success of, 123
Local history programs at: Pikes Peak Library District (PPLD), 77
Local referendums, 97–101; bond issues, 99–100; increasing statutory limitations, 98–99; revenue entitlements, 100–101; tax limitation overrides, 98
Los Angeles Public Library: foundations grants, 96; public referendum and, 101
Louisville Public Library, 83

Magazine subscription, donated, 75–76
Major capital campaigns, 94–97; community foundations, 96–97; family foundations, 96; library foundations, 96
Major marketing campaign themes, 88–93; building facility, 90–92; channels beyond print collection, 89; collection excellence, 89; community building, 92–93; diversity, 92; excellence, 93; new technology funding, 89; public programming, 90

Malaysia, 7–8
MARC, 35
Marketing, 57. *See also* Major marketing campaign themes
Mason, B., 67
Mason, M.G., 28
Massachusetts Campus Compact, 56
Matching gift, 85, 93–94
Media relations, 44–45
Memphis Public Library, 84
Memphis Public Library Information Center, 65
Metropolitan Group, 97, 104
Minneapolis Public Library, 85
Minnesota Council of Nonprofits, 103
Mission, developing personal, 22
Mission statement, library, 22
MIT library, 85
Mixed revenues approach, 121
Morgan, E.L., 60
Multnomah County Library, 101
Museums, 46
Must visit list, 115
MyLibrary, 68, 75, 124–26
My-space, 67
Myths, about libraries, 11–15; anyone can run library, 12; funding, 12; government funding, 13–14; librarians no longer needed, 12; librarian as manager, 12–13; nongovernment funding, 14–15; volunteers, 12

Naming opportunities, 91
National Center for Educational Statistics, 23
National Endowment for the Humanities, 77, 90
National Football League, 76
National Foundation Center, 47, 78
National Foundation Directory, 78

National Library Week (ALA), 115, 123
National Poetry Week, 30
Natrona County Public Library (NCPL), 95
Natural stakeholders, 31
Nesbitt, J., 88
New York Library Association (NYLA), 69
No Child Left Behind, 100
Nongovernmental organizations (NGOs), 33
Nongovernment funding, myths about, 14–15
Nonmonetary resources, 113
Nontax funds, 113
Normative reeducation, 24
Norway, 137

Oakland Public Library, 75
Office of Information Technology Project (OITP; ALA's), 36
Online book discussion, 126
Online Computer Library Center (OCLC), 31, 36, 38, 60, 69, 122
Online fundraising, 84–86, 96–97
Open *vs.* closed system, 48–49
Orphan books, 83–84
OurLibrary, 126–28
Overdue fines, 78

Panda syndrome, 7
Parent-teacher association (PTA), 73
Personnel budget, reducing, 35
Personnel management, 41
Peters, T., 124
Phoenix, Arizona Public Library, 77
Photocopying services, 77–78
Physically challenged users, 92
Pikes Peak Library District (PPLD): branding at, 58; change management at, 41–42; Community Information Systems, 30;

community survey by, 8–9;
  effectiveness and efficiency
  of, 16; foundation grants,
  96; local history programs
  at, 77; national ranking of,
  23; staff development at,
  18, 56
Placentia Public Library, 79
Planned Program Budgeting,
  17
Plaques, donor, 75
Podcast, 67
Poderis, T., 68
Poetry Ladies, 31
Policy, clarifying and
  codifying, 18
Political savvy, developing,
  118–20
Poster, as communication
  tool, 29–31, 52
Presentations, 25–26;
  communication skills,
  25–26; community
  organization, 72–73; use of
  audiovisuals in, 73
Press release, 64–65
Print media, 65–66
Private funding campaigns,
  93–94
Procedures, clarifying and
  codifying, 18
Product/service donation,
  76
Proposal, starter funding,
  121
Proposition 13 (CA), 97–98
ProQuest, 61
Public Benefits Valuation
  Study, 103–4
Public guardian, 83
Publicity sources, 114
Public Library Association
  (PLA), 23, 49, 60, 69
Public Library of Charlotte
  and Mecklenburg County,
  29, 137
Public Library Planning
  Process (ALA), 8
Public programming, 52, 74,
  76, 90
Public relations, 44, 52–53,
  56, 58, 62

Radio, 65–66
Rampart Library District,
  101
Recognition program, for
  formal support groups, 56
Recombinant library, 39, 88,
  91
Referendums, running
  campaign for, 101–7;
  budget for campaign,
  107–8; case statement, 103;
  closing out, 110;
  consultants, 106;
  door-to-door campaigning,
  108–9; endorsements,
  106–7; feedback, 110;
  Go-to-Team expansion,
  103–4; legal authority for
  plan, 102–3; opposition,
  109; polling, 105–6;
  request for proposal, 106;
  separate campaign
  committee, 105; speaker's
  bureau, 108; target swing
  voters, 107; telephone
  banks, 109; volunteers,
  108–9
Relationships, angels, 43, 47,
  94; communication
  differences, 45–46;
  cultivating, 45–48, 116–17;
  development department of
  parent organization, 46;
  devils, 47–48; library
  schools, 46; local
  foundations, 47; muscle
  people, 47; museums, 46
Remainder trusts, 79
Reputation building, 121
Right to Work Act, 37
Roadmap to Learning 2.0, 41
Rumor mill, minimizing
  negative, 17

San Francisco Foundation,
  95
San Francisco library system,
  community survey by,
  9–10
San Francisco Public Library
  (SFPL), 33; branding
  campaign at, 58–59;
  educating staff at, 18–19;
  funding, 14–15, 33, 46–47,
  59; legal authority for
  building project at, 102;
  media relations, 44–45;
  national ranking of, 23;
  NML project, 37, 40–41,
  62–63; poetry project,
  31–32; product donation,
  50, 76; public programming
  by FOL at, 90; scholarships
  for nonlibrarian staff at, 43;
  special collections at, 72,
  84; staff training at, 40–41;
  stakeholder alliances, 50;
  testimonials use in funding,
  62–63
San Jose State University,
  SLIS, 7, 67, 128
Scandinavia, 6–7
Scholastic Books, Inc., 74
Second Life, 67, 128
Seed money, government
  sources for, 96
Self-service model, 37
Services donations, 94
Shafer, S., 62
Silent auction, 74
Slate card, 107
Small community foundation
  grants, 78
Soft funding, 124
South Africa, 7
Speaker's bureau, 108
Sponsored book fairs, 74
St. Louis Public Library,
  103–4
St. Mary's County, Maryland
  library, 74
Staff: educating and
  informing, 18–19; as
  formal support group, 56
Stakeholders: communicating
  with, 6, 10; expectations of,
  5–7; identifying, 10;
  natural, 31. *See also*
  Elected officials
State funding, 80–81
Steinbruner, J.D., 24
Stephens, M., 124
Storytelling, 27
Story time, 76

Strategic development plan, 42, 114; development outline checklist, 136–38; planning as cyclical and continuous, 113; time issues, 112, 136; worksheet sample, 130–36
Stretch gifts, 92
Survey, community, 8–10
Swing voters, 107

Talent, employee, 121–22
Talent, outside: experts, 117; other library Web sites, 118; passionate persons, 118
Tattered Cover Book Store, 85
Tax funds, 113
Tax limitation overrides, 98
Team building, 39–40
Technology: effect on communication, 40; funding for, 89
Telephone banks, 109
Television, as communication tool, 65–67, 76
Testimonials, 62–63, 92
Toolkit for Advocacy, 49

Toronto Public Library, 85
Trust, 40, 93

UCLA libraries, 85
United Kingdom, 5, 100
University of Wisconsin School of Library and Information Science, 90
User fees, 77
Users, 29; change in, 35; physically challenged, 92

Values, developing personal, 22
Vancouver Public Library (WA), 101
Venable, A.A., Jr., 88
Virtual Donor Wall, 125
Virtual library, 122
Virtual Village Communication Center (VVCC), 137
Vision, developing personal, 22
Vision statement, library, 22
Visual Map of working relationships, 129
Volunteers, 113; for book sales, 73; formal support groups, 55; myths about, 12

Wales, 101
Washington Office (ALA), 82
WebJunction, 41, 60, 69
Westerville Ohio Public Library, 97
WiFi, 88
Williams, J.F., 12
Wills and bequests, 79
Winnipeg Library Foundation Library System, 118
Wisconsin Library Association, 100
Wyoming, state funding in, 81
Wyoming State Library (WSL), 54, 74

Yahoo, 125–26
Yale University, 104
Yiotis, K., 56–57
Young adult (YA) programming, 90

Zaslow, J., 5
Zelienople (PA) Area Public Library, 74
Zero Based Budgeting, 17